"Faced with anxiety and depression in record numbers, too many young people today feel the church hasn't prepare them for the tough questions life creates. Too many trendy writers respond with appealing answers that sound pretty but don't match reality. Rachael Dymski's deep, compelling writing remarries beauty and truth to help readers face a world that is unmistakably tragic but, like every one of us, inescapably part of the divine story."

—Brian Brown, director, The Anselm Society

"*Anxiety Interrupted* is a treasured guide for those of us who struggle with worry. Rachael Dymski's chapter on motherhood in which she shares her fears, first about becoming a mother and then about raising her daughter in a fallen world, will speak to mothers at all stages. Rachael asks a question many mothers want to ask—*Am I responsible for my child's salvation?* Rachael writes honestly and tenderly, encouraging us to see anxiety as a gift that proves we're alive. Her salve is the reminder that God is good. This book provides strong encouragement to those struggling with anxiety. Through its gentle pages we learn it's okay to question as long as we remember God is the answer."

—Julianne Palumbo, author of *50/50*, founder and
editor-in-chief of *Mothers Always Write*

"In a Christian culture skilled at dodging the hard questions lingering behind anxiety, stress, and depression, Rachael Dymski invites us to lean in and embrace them. With the tender touch of gentle curiosity, Rachael draws us into the invitation to live the questions themselves. As we seek God in the midst of the unknown and unfinished of our lives, we find courage, freedom, and joy-filled inspiration to continue along the transformational, question-packed journey of life with God."

—Mary Vandel Young, MDiv, executive director of JourneyMates

"I believe good books are food for the soul, and Rachael Dymski's *Anxiety Interrupted* doesn't disappoint! If you have ever struggled with anxiety, then you know the terror of panic and the paralyzing fear that comes unannounced and uninvited—in public, at home, even in the quiet of our thoughts. The feelings of doubt and lostness that accompany anxiety can bring physical symptoms that interrupt our lives and rock our beliefs. Rachael's words are refreshingly real, and you immediately feel a warmth and connection with her. You feel a sense of tearful relief that you have finally found a friend who understands the silent, mysterious journey you've been hiding; you've found someone who is asking the same hard questions. For every person who wrestles in the middle of the night with the crushing intensity of anxiety, Rachael's words will be oxygen to your soul. For every person who struggles to make sense of anxiety in the context of our faith and who has more questions than answers, this book will be a source of comfort and strength. Understanding that anxiety can even be an unlikely gift recalibrates your thoughts and will refresh your spirit. Whether you're a teenager, a new mother, a struggling parent, or a successful professional, Rachael's story will bring truth, calm, and hope for your own tomorrow and for those in your life who seek your counsel."

—Anne Deeter Gallaher, owner and CEO of Deeter Gallaher Group LLC and author of *Women in High Gear and Students in High Gear*

anxiety
interrupted

anxiety interrupted

Invite God's Peace into Your Questions, Doubts & Fears

RACHAEL DYMSKI

NEW HOPE®
PUBLISHERS

An imprint of Iron Stream Media
Birmingham, Alabama

New Hope® Publishers
5184 Caldwell Mill Rd.
St. 204-221
Hoover, AL 35244
NewHopePublishers.com
An imprint of Iron Stream Media

© 2019 by Rachael Dymski
All rights reserved. First printing 2019.
Printed in the United States of America.

No part of this publication may be reproduced, stored in a retrieval system, or transmitted in any form or by any means—electronic, mechanical, photocopying, recording, or otherwise—without the prior written permission of the publisher.

New Hope Publishers serves its authors as they express their views, which may not express the views of the publisher.

Library of Congress Cataloging-in-Publication Data

Names: Dymski, Rachael, 1989- author.
Title: Anxiety interrupted : invite God's peace into your questions, doubts, and fears / Rachael Dymski.
Description: First [edition]. | Birmingham : New Hope Publishers, 2019.
Identifiers: LCCN 2018050134 | ISBN 9781563091384 (permabind)
Subjects: LCSH: Anxiety—Religious aspects—Christianity. | Trust in God—Christianity.
Classification: LCC BV4908.5 .D96 2019 | DDC 248.8/6—dc23
LC record available at https://lccn.loc.gov/2018050134

All Scripture quotations, unless otherwise indicated, are taken from the Holy Bible, New International Version®, NIV®. Copyright © 1973, 1978, 1984, 2011 by Biblica, Inc.™ Used by permission of Zondervan. All rights reserved worldwide. www.zondervan.com The "NIV" and "New International Version" are trademarks registered in the United States Patent and Trademark Office by Biblica, Inc.™

Scripture quotations marked (ESV) are from The Holy Bible, English Standard Version® (ESV®), copyright © 2001 by Crossway, a publishing ministry of Good News Publishers. Used by permission. All rights reserved.

ISBN-13: 978-1-56309-138-4
Ebook ISBN: 978-1-56309-141-4

1 2 3 4 5—23 22 21 20 19

To my mom and dad, who held my questions first;
to Andrew, who brought them to light;
to the Fellows and Dinner Club,
for always making room.

Contents

This little book would never have come about without the help and patience of a great number of people.

Thank you to New Hope Publishers, for your time, patience, and kindness with this manuscript. Every department has been so wonderful to work with, and I truly feel like this work has been handled with great care and consideration. Thank you specifically to Reagan Jackson and Ramona Richards for your keen editorial eyes and to Tina and Meredith for all your amazing work in the marketing department.

Thank you to Dan Balow and Steve Laube Agency for believing in my writing and standing behind me this whole way.

Thank you to my classmates and professors at Chatham University for teaching me to listen to the words.

Thank you to the people of Liberti Church for being a home for Andrew and me in Pennsylvania. We love you and are so grateful for the ways you have challenged and encouraged us.

To my family: thank you, Mom, for being my biggest and best cheerleader, and Dad, for engaging any topic. Thank you to my siblings and their spouses, Laura, Mike, Amy, Kevin, Matt, and Liz, for living out these questions with me, as family and as friends. Thank you to Jim and Lisa for watching my daughter, providing meals, and getting me through the thick of this writing. Thank you, Andrew, for everything else. This book is as much yours as it is mine.

Questions, Doubts, and Fears

What do you think of when you think about the ocean?

Though my childhood home near Buffalo, New York, is nowhere near it, I grew up at the ocean in a lot of ways. I'm part of an island family. We can trace our family tree back to the 1500s, when we inhabited what is now known as England's Channel Islands.

My mother was raised on a small, sea-locked patch of land fourteen miles off the coast of France called Jersey, an island that, in theory, belongs to the English Crown but, in lifestyle and culture, bears greater resemblance to its French counterpart. It's the kind of place a nomad would visit, because as soon as you step onto the island's shores, you immediately feel as though you are part of something. The island brims with turbulent history: for centuries its power passed back and forth among nations. If you put your ear to the ground, you could still hear the hurried footsteps of the Vikings, the victory calls of King John's men in 1204, and the eerie hush brought over by Nazi Germany. And yet, all this time, there were still cows to milk and potatoes to grow, so Jersey maintained its down-to-earth quaint quality that brings thousands of tourists to the island today.

The island, spanning an area of only forty-five square miles, boasts a population of nearly one hundred thousand while designating more than 50 percent of its land to agriculture. Since the liberation of Jersey from Nazi Germany at the end of World War II, the island has become something of a "posh" place to live, its picturesque beaches and breathtaking views beckoning the rich from all over the world. At Jersey's core, though, hidden to the tourists and foreigners, is the life and society of the "Jerseyman" and the "Jerseywoman." Historically, it's an agricultural society, comprised of plowing potatoes as the sea salt sticks to sweat, of attending hog roasts with brimming hats and homespun dresses, of chickens, wild rabbit, and the scent of lavender that the wind carries across the cliffs. It's a nautical society, one where talk of the tides spills over with greetings, where mussels don't get fresher than right off the boat in time for market, where islanders managed to survive the war on seaweed soups and scavenged crabs. This is where my mom was raised alongside tides of more than thirty feet, lowering picnic baskets down cliff walls to beaches for lunches on Sundays, surfing in the waves of St. Ouen's Bay, and sailing with friends in and out of the coves.

My mom grew up and left the island, married a man from England, and moved to America, but it's still a part of her and who she is—how can a place like that not be? So many of my childhood memories take place at the ocean in Jersey. The island is home to some of the biggest tidal waves in the world that can rise and fall nearly forty feet up and down the coast. At La Rocque, the beach where my grandparents lived, when the tides receded, we'd look in the shallow pools for anemones, fish, prawns, and crabs. We couldn't look too long though, or we'd find ourselves with the water back up to our ankles, and then our knees, and we'd run for safer, higher sand. There, we spread out on picnic blankets and ate cheese and tomato sandwiches while the sun dried our skin. I would watch the wisps of white hair that grew straight up on my grandfather's head, thinking, if he'd let me, I'd braid them together so they all moved in one direction.

How many days did I have like that as a child? Five? Fifty? I don't know if it matters. Those days soaked into my skin and shaped my preliminary views of the ocean: untamable, life giving, life taking, unconquerable. And how I fit into all of that I am still trying to work out.

Here are some facts about the ocean: it covers approximately 70 percent of the world we live in and remains largely undiscovered. It is possible that in addition to the more than two hundred thousand marine species that have been identified, there could be up to two million more species that have not been identified. The ocean is pulled by the moon and the sun, and it contains more energy than the rest of the earth several times over. The ocean is simultaneously a place of life and a place of death, a place of light and beauty, and a place of intense darkness. I was both comforted and perturbed by that as I grew older, but I have never stopped being fascinated by this body of water.

We have family members who played a role in the evacuation of Dunkirk, the beach made famous for its pivotal role in World War II. Then it was littered with helmets, dark boots, growling stomachs, and hands still fresh with the blood of their enemies and the blood of their friends. The trapped British Army, holders of the world's largest empire a stone's throw away from defeat, were surrounded by German troops led by a man no one took seriously on every side. The free world teetered in the arms of boys too young and boys too old, and men who were never made to carry such a weight.

The free world was kept on course that day not only by military ships and large machines but by ordinary people—some in my own family tree—afloat on private vessels and their own courage, sailing into enemy territory not in military uniform but as ordinary people, to save the face of their army.

Maybe the ocean for those soldiers, after they were rescued, was like a safety blanket—protecting them the way a wall would. Maybe before they were rescued it was also a wall, but one they couldn't penetrate without help. The channel that separated England from the continent worked as a giant moat, buying time and strategy in the face of Hitler's army. Whatever they thought about the ocean, it didn't change the fact about what the ocean actually *was*.

The year after I graduated college, I moved to North Carolina for a postgraduate program and walked through some of the hardest months of my life. I was away from my friends, my family, and my fiancé, and in that year, I experienced death in a way I never had before. It was a year of questioning for me: Why does suffering happen? Why do bad things happen? Is the universe controlled by a good God or by cold chaos? Can I trust God?

I finished the program, married my husband three weeks later, and flew to a tropical island for our honeymoon. At night, we walked through the sand down to the beach. With no lights around us but the moon and the stars, the sounds of the ocean were amplified. What sounded like gentle waves in the daytime became bigger and scarier, sinister, repetitive slaps at night. The ocean, which had always been a place of inspiration and intrigue for me, suddenly felt only ominous, too capable of doing harm. I had come out of one of the hardest years of my life, a year when my reformed theology was shaken to its core and I was scared of dying, scared of living, scared of anything outside my own skin. I was hyper-aware that I was living because of the death around me, and I felt raw-real, in a way I didn't like. I wanted to hide, to medicate, to lose myself in a book or in trivial projects because I could not face anything heavier.

What's true of the ocean? It's been thought about so many different ways by so many different people, and it is still vastly unexplored. Does the way people think about it change the way it actually is?

The ocean, in many ways, represents my relationship with God. He is unknowable except in the ways He has chosen to make Himself known—fascinating, amazing, fear-inducing, awe-inspiring. People have thought about God in so many different ways, and it shapes the way they view everything about themselves and everything that happens in their lives.

It is the trying to understand God, trying to understand myself, and trying to piece together my life and my faith that has been the source, equally, of great anxiety and great joy in my life. I have not yet learned how to hold in both hands that God is sovereign and that people die of hunger. I have not been able to reconcile why we live in a world where pain and pleasure mingle so closely; I do not understand the eternal implications of this life. I am an anxious person because there are questions I cannot answer about God, about life, about people, and about myself.

But I am also a Christian. So by definition, shouldn't that mean I'm not anxious?

Do anxiety and faith ever intersect? Can you live as a Christian when you struggle with both? How do call yourself a Christian when you are riddled with worry? How do you live by faith when you are skittish like the sparrow, quick to flee at the first sign of trouble?

One of the easiest ways to disable a person is to make them anxious. I am not talking about an anxiety disorder, a diagnosable medical disorder that should be treated by doctors, therapy, medication, or a combination thereof. I am talking about sweaty hands, sleepless nights, worry, and questions that are part of everyday life, more so now, it seems, than ever. I am talking about the discomfort to our bodies and spirits caused by the mind racing faster than mouth or logic, worrying about tomorrow, worrying about all we don't know, worrying about what could happen.

I know this about myself as I look back on the edges and corners of my life: the lines, so often, are drawn and defined by anxiety. I also know that I am a Christian, and therefore, much of my life is defined by peace and joy. How do I reconcile the two? How do I respond to people who tell me *real* Christians don't struggle with anxiety?

Is it a sin? Can it be stopped?

Anxiety is a fierce, irrational pest, defying all logic and reason—or maybe it is the only emotion that is completely reasonable. Its origins, I think, lie in what we don't know. When I was little, I was afraid of the dark. As an adult, I am still afraid of the dark, but now that darkness is cancer, illness, the future, and death.

Some people, though, feel anxious and worried even when they are perfectly safe. They worry about what *might* come to be, what could but hasn't yet passed. They have unanswerable questions and fears about God, about faith, and about suffering. Maybe a life event has plunged them into a well of worry. Maybe they suffer from panic attacks. Maybe their worry has become so great that they are afraid to leave their own front door, even when the sun shines brightly outside.

This kind of worry is paralyzing, debilitating. I know because I have lived it. And I have also learned many Christians have quietly walked the same path as me, suffering in silent cells of panic because even more than their anxiety, they are afraid to talk about it. The answer, after all, in popular Christian culture, in reformed circles, in Pentecostal, charismatic circles, is *I'll pray for you. Have more faith. God is sovereign.*

And while I know the theology, I cannot reconcile God being sovereign with this horrible thing happening in my life. I'm not asking for the right answer to be written down on a piece of paper, and I'm not looking to be impressed or outwitted by something recited from a book. I want to know, *how do I move forward in this moment?* When I cannot hold in both hands that God is sovereign and that people die of hunger without beginning to think that one must somehow negate the other, how do I continue in my professed faith? How do I make my faith more than meaningless words? Is there a purpose to wading through muddy waters, to wrestling with these questions, to openly admitting anxiety and doubt and then sitting with the discomfort of the silence?

I see two threads weaving my life together, equally strong, equally present: anxiety and faith. What does it mean that God has not taken away my anxiety? Heaven knows I have asked for it to be removed. What does it say about God, about sin, about the way we choose to look at struggle in the Christian church, if I don't know a Christian who *doesn't* desperately need the gospel to be a reality in their lives because without it, and maybe even with it, they are a wreck? Doesn't

> How do I move forward in this moment?

my anxiety remind me of God? Hasn't it been the source of the most remarkable growth in my walk with Christ?

The church is often strangely quiet on the subjects of mental issues: anxiety, depression, resentment, pride. As Christians, there is a tendency to think that if we are anxious, we are doing something wrong. We must not have enough faith. We must not be worshipping God the right way. We must be asking too many questions. But this mentality only heaps guilt on those who suffer from anxiety. It also closes off room for discussion. We are afraid to talk about our anxiety because we do not want to be seen as weak.

If that is not true, if we are not weak, then why are we anxious?

One of the most influential books I have ever read is *A Severe Mercy* by Sheldon Vanauken. In it, he says, "To believe with certainty . . . one has to begin by doubting."

In this world, good and evil, joy and suffering, seem to exist so painfully close together, almost touching, almost intertwined. It is hard, when really living in this world, to get very far believing in a Sovereign God without asking some very difficult questions. The thing about God, I'm learning, is that He is a great mystery. And He might let us live with some of these hard questions for days, years, centuries, not because He is angry with us, but because He is using this space inside of our questions to make us think, to expose our hearts, and to ultimately pursue us.

For years I was embarrassed by my questions and doubts. I thought that if I were really a Christian, I would have left my questioning behind. I would have figured out the answers. But it seems to me the longer I am a Christian and the more I read the Bible, the more questions I have.

This makes sense, though, doesn't it? If God is an overwhelming mystery, then it makes sense the more we read and learn of Him in His revealed Word the more questions we stir up. Because we long for everything to be made right, for reconciliation with our lives and our theology, and rightly so, because we are approaching the day where God *will* one day reconcile all things to Himself.

What I have learned through my own journey with anxiety—in my faith, my friendships, my marriage, my calling, my understanding, and the church—is this: it is not in the Lord's nature to have us question in vain. He uses our struggles to draw us closer to Him. In the midst of all of our questions, we can sometimes feel as though we are free falling through the universe. But He gives us promises and understanding to stand on. In the ugly depths of my anxiety, I have found treasures of hope that I will one day lay before the throne in the presence of all His angels because I will know something of suffering, and something of His love, that even angels do not.

If God is sovereign, then there is a reason for the questions. There is a reason for the anxiety, and none of this is meaningless. We can walk forward and explore this murkiness because *He is light*, and no matter how dark or scary, He will not leave us where we are.

Sometimes the questions must be *lived.* The following pages are my wandering thoughts from the small window through which I have lived and wondered and asked. But my story is not complete because my life is not complete. Your story may be similar to mine or it may be entirely different, but it is my hope that if nothing else, this book will give you space. I pray it gives you the space for room and quiet, to ask, to wonder, to imagine and experience the goodness of God. I pray it will help you wade a little bit through your own murky waters and make sense of the days of your life and what they contain.

Whatever we feel, we *are* safe as we ask our questions and work through our anxiety—because Jesus will always bring us through. He must: for He is all we have.

CHAPTER 1

The Questions, the Gift, and the Promise

The mind that is not baffled is not employed
The impeded stream is the one that sings.

—Wendell Berry, *The Real Work*

A friend told me once that often, the very thing we think will separate us from God actually brings us closer to him than anything else could. For me, that thing has been my questions.

If I had it my way, I would not be a person who asked questions. I would be a person who lived life with my nose to the ground, never wondering about anything, never questioning what was put in front of me. I would choose not to go digging through my own soul to find my doubts and fears piled up, desperately needing attention. I would choose to be a person who took the world and my faith at face value, who could just say, "This is the way it is," wipe my hands, and have that be that.

Truth is, not many people are actually like that. I've met people who question their faith and are comforted by the growth they find in their searching. I most definitely am not. Even if the doubts are ultimately for my good, the questioning is painful. I often asked God why He made me the way He did. Why did He give me so many doubts and fears? Why is my heart so prone to being afraid? Why does it take so much for me to trust Him?

For years, I thought these questions were a sign something was wrong with me. I thought something wasn't clicking, with me and Christianity. I thought that if I could just read something a little harder, pray a little more, or sing a little louder, those questions would just fall into place somewhere behind me, dropping into a bucket where I would never pull them out again.

I would have been content to leave my questions behind, had they been content to do so with me. But they seemed to follow me everywhere I went. I would wake up in the night thinking about the concept of existence, wondering why there are so many humans on the planet, why we like to watch other humans on television for entertainment, why we are so fascinated with ourselves. I would read Christian tracts and books with the nagging feeling that popular Christian culture does not have a correct understanding of God. I would listen to prayers at church and wonder about the way we are meant to pray, about what prayer is, about what it all means if God already knows everything we are about to say. I would wonder how, with billions of people who have existed, God knows my name or anything about me. I would wonder, if He didn't want us to have anything to do with sin, why He would allow it to exist in the first place.

It is only recently that I have begun to see these questions as gifts. I see them as gifts because of the way they push me. They push me into Scripture, into prayer, into relationship, and into humility in a way maybe nothing else has. This very thing I thought separated me from God pushed me toward Him because I had nowhere else to go with my questions and fears. What I've learned about this anxiety and about these questions is all of it is a gift.

There are other gifts, of course, some of which I am aware of and some of which I may not know for years or for eternity to come. Here is one I know about already though: the questions and the anxiety have shown me that I am alive.

"Well, I bet you cried the first time you were born too. It means you're alive," says the reverend in Marilynne Robinson's novel *Lila*. It's the emotions, the physical representation of those emotions, that show us what we are. When you are so anxious you feel like you cannot breathe, like you cannot get another breath in, that is when you know you're breathing more poignantly than any other moment. Maybe there is this world and there is the other world, but there are holes between the two all around us, a thinly made curtain. And sometimes it is the sound of a solitary cello, sometimes it is the mockingbird, the sound of a firework, the steady rush of a stream, that give us a quick glimpse into the whole other world that lives parallel to ours and makes us more aware than we were a moment before. Maybe anxiety is like this too. Anxiety, maybe, is an awareness of the darkness, the flap of another curtain that reminds us this world is not what it should be, and I am afraid, for my life or for another's life. I am craving certainty, and I do not have it.

> Anxiety, maybe, is an awareness of the darkness, the flap of another curtain that reminds us this world is not what it should be.

Anxiety makes us aware of the brightness of the sun, of the vastness of the sky. We become aware we are small, one of billions, and that our world is one planet in the solar system, the solar system is one part of a galaxy, and the galaxy is one small corner of this whole universe. We are so insignificant, and yet we are also complex, composed, the perfect balance of skin and bone, with hearts that beat and minds that think, and so what does this all mean?

This is the gift: the reminder of our smallness and complexity. Most of the time, we like to make ourselves in charge of our worlds. We let our worlds become consumed by our social media, our schedule, our friend group, and we think that is what defines us. We don't know what our lives mean or what happens when we die, so we ignore it by making our lives small and containable. Those who are anxious, though, are aware that is impossible. To be anxious is to be aware that there is much, much more in the world and in this life than we know.

In this world, we have the words *alive* and *dead*, but I wonder if we've mixed it up somewhere along the way. Are the dead truly dead? Or are they more alive and aware than we are? Do they finally know about the things we wonder? And what would they say about our lives, the way we make them small?

The Gift in All Things

Creepy was the word that came to my mind when I found our first house online. It wasn't the word I would have wanted to describe my first home, not even in the top ten, but the house was in our price range, so I sent it to my husband at work.

"Let's see it!" he responded enthusiastically.

We were currently living in the old servants' quarters of a Pittsburgh mansion on a university campus, rumored to be haunted and filled with ghosts. I was a resident director and a graduate student, and too old, in my opinion, to be scared of an old, dusty, creaky place like the apartment we lived in, but after a few nights there by myself with thunderstorms and wind howling on the glass and down the chimney, I was ready for something with a little less history.

Andrew promised me this place had potential. I thought, there is no harm in just *seeing* it, so I braved the overgrown rhododendron bushes, the stained carpets that gave off a musty odor, and the badly painted, puke-colored walls. My husband stood in that room in another place and time, on Christmas morning, with a fire in the stove, soft colored walls, hardwood floors, and a fat Norwegian fir in front of the window. He did that with every room, until I saw the butcher block countertops in the kitchen, white tile in the bathroom, updated appliances, a groomed backyard, and in a moment of complete insanity, said yes, let's do it. We found ourselves the brand new owners of the most run-down house in the neighborhood.

I knew transforming a run-down house into a home where we could live, be comfortable, and settle, would not be easy. I dreaded the construction, the dust, sleeping on a mattress in the middle of the living room, and ripping layers of linoleum out of the kitchen.

What I did not expect about remodeling a home was to find the gift in it.

Houses are storytellers too, maybe the best of them. A house holds everything a person needs to make a life, and between its walls it harbors joys, sorrows, first steps, Christmases. It harbors the laundry, the dishes, the beds, the tidying, the constant decluttering needed to provide our families with places to be themselves. A house encompasses all of the ordinary everyday-ness that makes up all we are and will become. As we uncovered layers of the floor, as we scraped up wallpaper and ripped out cabinets, we captured remnants of the owners who lived there before us. Though built just after World War II, our house has only had one other owner. He married a German girl who loved flowers, which we knew because the whole house was covered in floral wallpaper beneath an awful, off-white paint. We found little notecards, invitations, and journal entries beneath floorboards and behind cabinets and were able to piece together little snippets of the full life that was lived before us: the car that parked every night in our driveway and the children who sat around the dining room table. And I realized then that we were doing the same thing. We chose this house to hold our memories before we even made them. This house was going to tell our story. And that was a gift.

A friend told me once that there is a gift in all things. Even the things that seem bad, unwanted, and horrible can be a gift.

The feelings that have surrounded my anxiety for years have been shame and fear. Even more than the anxiety itself, I've been afraid to tell people about it, to let them know what grips me in the night. I haven't been able to view it as a gift. But I wonder about the person I am becoming, the things I am learning about God and His love for us, and if that is in spite of the anxiety or because of it. I don't think I would have asked questions if I never had anxiety. I don't think I would have wondered. I don't think I would have the empathy I do now for people who feel like they are stuck under water with a weight— addiction, depression, anger, or loneliness—and can't swim to the

> I don't think I would have asked questions if I never had anxiety. I don't think I would have wondered.

top for air, because I have felt like that too. I wonder if maybe God knew these questions are what it would take for me to know Him more. And so that, and all the other things that come with my questions and my anxiety, is a gift.

The following chapters address the specific ways in which I've experienced big questions and anxiety in my life and some of the ways I have come to understand them as gifts. Gratitude, for me, has been the biggest antidote for my anxiety.

So awareness, of the anxiety and the gratitude, is another gift. It has prevented me from living a boxed up, container life, from taking the conventional way, from living life unaware that I am living, that I consist of cells made up perfectly to accommodate breath, lungs, oxygen, blood, a beating ensemble with a tune. The awareness makes me think maybe the worst thing isn't to have cancer, or to lose a loved one, or to be alone, or disliked, or any of these other things that worry me. Maybe the worst thing would be to live with my nose to the ground, never knowing any pain or fear that could make me ask why. Maybe those questions push away at the dam between *here* and *there*. Maybe to be both alive and aware that I am living is part of what I am here for.

The following chapters are threefold. They first address different areas of my life where I have experienced anxiety, fear, and doubt and the questions I have asked specific to those areas. Then they explain the promises of God I have been able to hold to through my doubts and fears. Lastly, they explain the ways I have been able to or am learning to see each area as a gift or how I have experienced God's grace in each area. As I have said, the book is not complete because my life is not finished, so my wrestling in each is not done with. I am wading through, and my prayer as you read is that you will be encouraged to keep wading through your own life. May you know through your own wanderings that you too are alive.

CHAPTER 2

When I'm Anxious about God

You have been given questions to which you cannot be given answers. You will have to live them out—perhaps a little at a time.

—Wendell Berry, *Jayber Crow*

One of my favorite stories as a child was Chicken Little. We used to read it sometimes, in that gap between dinner and bed when we suddenly realized the rope of the day was about to run out and we had to squeeze all those fun things in before it was time to sleep. We had a red-burgundy carpet in our living room, the kind that would seem awful today, something new homeowners would likely take a look at and say, "Who on earth would ever choose a red carpet?" But to me that carpet looked like royalty, and it felt plush and luxurious to lay on. So I stretched out on that carpet with my siblings, all laughing at silly Henny Penny, who was convinced the sky was falling. Didn't they know anything about the way air worked, we asked each other against the backdrop of our parents talking and scraping dishes in the kitchen. Doesn't she know the sky couldn't actually fall?

I wonder, when I look at my childhood, why I have so many questions. My childhood was, in many ways, idyllic. My parents had their four children in five years and a nice home with lots of grass and a meadow that stretched behind it and turned golden in the evening hours. I grew up with two believing parents and three siblings who all became Christians. We traveled back and forth to

England to visit our extended family, and my brother and I would invent things like portable playhouses—shoe boxes with plates taped to the lid—to entertain us on flights. It wasn't a traumatic or unfair upbringing. I was given, as a child, the gift of time—to be outside, to get to know my siblings, to be creative, to think about the world. Maybe it was the time that gave me the questions. Maybe it was the time to realize that not everyone had a life like mine.

One of the things I remember poignantly about my childhood is that my older sister had a lot of headaches. Though it felt like she got them all the time, she especially got them after exercising. I can remember riding our bikes to get ice cream after dinner in the summertime and my sister lying on the picnic table when we got there because she was in so much pain. For years doctors called it growing pains . . . until the eye doctor discovered the tumor in the back of her brain. My sister had emergency surgery the next day. We were told had her eye doctor not discovered it, the fluid buildup would have caused seizures, blindness, and other severe health problems within a few weeks.

It was, by all accounts, a miracle. God saved my sister, and praise God for that, because she is one of the dearest friends I've ever known. He protected her from what could have come next. My parents said God was sovereign, and even though that night before surgery I snuck out of bed into the hallway and watched my dad cry as he hunched over the stairs, I knew they believed what they told me.

I guess the unsettling part for me was I wasn't sure what I believed.

Why did God choose for this to happen to my sister? What was the point? Why not me? For the first time I recognized that our family, happy as it was, was not impenetrable. Bad things could happen to us. What would happen in the future? What did this mean about God? If something else, something worse, happened to our family, was He still good?

I felt that night like Henny Penny, with the sky splattering its weight all over my chest. Not silly Henny Penny. Silly me. How could I not know the weight of the air?

As Christians, what do we do when the sky falls?

I began having panic attacks in middle school. Anyone who has had one knows panic attacks are a mental game, but they manifest themselves physically. We know, logically, the sky is not falling, but our hearts are beating fit to burst, and the breaths don't come in or out like they should. I panic because I feel too small. I suddenly am aware of the incomprehensible largeness of the world around me, and it feels like it's too big, too much, to take in. I feel as though there is no way I could possibly be significant, and if I am not significant, how do I know God wants what is best for me?

My anxiety does not stem from wondering whether God exists. I know He exists. What are the chances, as C. S. Lewis once surmised, that we could have dreams, wishes, hopes, bigger than a world created by fluke? I look at a fingerprint, and I know God exists. What gives me anxiety is not knowing, or trusting, that God is good. I realized at ten years old that bad things could happen to people God loves. Did I not understand his love or was God's definition of love far different from my own?

My anxiety stems from a lack of control, from questions that have no answers. It grows when I am reminded that nothing in this world is certain but our death. It grows when strangers are killed, family members get sick, or friends die, and I cannot answer why. It grows when the actions around me point to a universe controlled not by a sovereign, loving God, but by cold, irrational chance, and when I feel as though I better watch out because it is coming for me next.

There are questions, yes, that have no answers, questions I may have to live with my entire life. But if I can't answer the questions that make me anxious, I wonder if I can pinpoint *why* they make me anxious. What is the cause of my anxiety? Why am I convinced the sky is falling when I know, factually, it is still up there? What do I do that feeds and waters my anxiety? How do I let it grow?

And finally, how can I make it stop?

The Question: Is He Good?

There are a lot of paths a person can take in the world, maybe as many as there are blades of grass or river bends. I don't know how much of it is instilled on a person or how much is inherent, but the fact is we are a sea of people comprised of paradoxes, emotion, logic, will, desire, and eventually something outside us tugs on one of those things to pull us in a direction.

How much do our life experiences shape who we become? I grew up in a Christian home, and so naturally, that faith is what I believed. My childhood was pleasant, and I was ten years old before I realized the world could be unfair to people. I didn't know what to do with that. Other people experience cruelty far earlier and more intensely than I did, and I think that shapes the people they become and the way they view the world. At one point during my childhood, we had a dear friend diagnosed with cancer as a high school student. I know many other children experience that word and its consequences far before I did, but my first reaction was to ask why. Did he want to get cancer? Did he ask for it? Did he like having cancer? And all that summer, while I slept to the sound of lawnmowers and woke to the smell of freshly cut grass, I lay in my bed feeling for lumps, for a cough, for a sign something wasn't right and that I had cancer too.

It sounds silly and ridiculous now, and not the type of memory that would mean anything but the illogical mind of a child, but I think in my own way, I was asking the question, is God good? Could I trust God when this friend of ours might not survive? And what if someone else I knew—my mom, or dad, or sibling—was next? In my opinion, cancer was never and could never be good. So what was a God who gave cancer?

This, more or less, is the question I asked throughout my adolescent years. Maybe, at the core, it's the question a lot of us ask, in our own ways and paths. Because of my upbringing, I knew, theologically, God was good. I knew He was sovereign. But did I trust that? And how could I reconcile it with the bad things that happened? More, how could I reconcile it with my own fear of bad things happening? I knew, theologically, that I was supposed to have faith and not doubt. But how does one do that, especially when you are in the moment and the questions and the doubt and the anxiety seem so big? How do you say, "Okay, fears, time to leave. You have no place here, because I am trusting God"?

I spent a summer during college in Guatemala at a home for neglected and abused girls. These weren't orphan girls. They were girls whose families couldn't, or wouldn't, care for them. I went to Latin

America with a camera and a journal. Sure, I would write about how these people had nothing but were so happy, something I had grown up hearing in the church. But that's not what I saw at all. These girls had and were desperate for more; they were hard, they were mean, they were cold and difficult to reach. They were bitter, and with good reason. What some of these girls had endured I hadn't even known was a possibility. So how do you take their experience and teach them about a good Father, when they have no context for what that is? How do you preach the gospel without imposing your own theology, and is the gospel stronger than your cultural context of it?

Over and over in the Bible, when God asked His people to do something, He prefaced it by saying to not be afraid. He knows we instinctively fear. *Don't be afraid, Moses—I am the God of your fathers. Don't be afraid, Joshua, for I will make you strong and courageous. Do not be afraid, David, for I will slay this giant for you. Do not be afraid, Hezekiah, for I am doing a new thing. Do not be afraid, Mary, through this pain and sorrow you will birth the world's redemption. Do not be afraid, Joseph, you are about to witness a great thing. Do not be afraid, shepherds, when you see the curtain of heaven's host peeled back; we bring you news of great joy. Do not be afraid, early church, for you have been given a spirit of sonship and not fear. Do not be afraid, John, though I am about to tell you how the world ends and begins again. For I hold the keys of death and hades in My hands, and I am God.*

Maybe the compassion of God is a lot deeper than ours—both for ourselves and for others. When we run to Him and say the world is a scary place, He doesn't laugh it off or tell us we are wrong. He doesn't say, *your theology should have taught you how to respond to that.* He says, *yes, it is a big and scary place, but I am bigger. Yes, what*

I am asking you to do is hard, but I will be strong for you. Yes, you will face days of pain and of brokenness, but I hold every one of your tears in a bottle, and it is my job to heal the broken and bind up their wounds. I am the first and the last and I surely will see you through every one of these temporary, pilgrim days. It's a comfort, that the only one who can see everything—who knows the true breadth of evil and sin and sees better than we do how strongly it grips and threatens to destroy us—tells us not to be afraid. So He really must be bigger than all of it.

Is He good? Is He good when bad things happen? Is He good when life or us or other people take our bodies in a direction that is broken and shattered and hard? Is He good when He doesn't take away our fears like we ask Him to, but He asks us to trust Him anyway? Is He good when we become bitter and angry about the things that have happened to us? Is He good, no matter what?

I believe the way we answer that question is fundamentally linked to who we become, especially when we deal with anxiety. If God is not good, then we are out for ourselves. We are the only ones, at the end of the day, who will protect ourselves, and we have to live like that. If He is good, though, then we can trust Him through the worst of it, and if He is good, He'll teach us, over time, to do that. If He is good, then He won't leave us where we are, and even though it might feel as though we aren't moving or growing in our trust or understanding, we'll look back ten years down the road and realize we aren't standing on the same stone we were then. If He is good, then even our fears can teach us about His

> If He is good, then even our fears can teach us about His character.

character. Even our fears are worthwhile because they push us to ask the questions that lead to life.

So God understands our fears; He acknowledges our fears, and then He asks us to push forward anyway. And He promises to be with us. Is that how you would define God? Here is the way God defines himself: Father, Shepherd, Healer, Counselor. The Bible is full of bringing the outsiders in, in caring for orphans and widows. God cares for the weak, and the Bible is full of those stories.

That eases the weight of the questions a little—to know someone else is carrying them with me. Maybe this is what the psalmist meant in Psalm 46 when he says God is my refuge and my strength, our ever present help in trouble—so let the mountains fall into the heart of the sea, let the earth shake, because there is a river who makes glad the people of God, and that river runs in me—and it is good.

Is He good? That is a question I have asked my whole life. My answer, after years of wrestling, is a yes, however small and feeble at times that yes might be. I have read the Bible, and I cannot ignore what it says, nor can I ignore the evidence of God's faithfulness in my own life. I'll take hold of this knowledge and experience like a torch and let it guide my steps as I walk forward into all these things I cannot understand or reconcile. He is good.

Conversations with a "Bad Catholic"

During graduate school, I taught creative writing at nursing homes. I loved getting to escape campus and cell phones and the urgency of life for a little bit and sit with people who were no longer hurried about anything. We would do a writing activity, and then we'd spend most of the hour talking. Some people told me the same stories again and again, and it would amaze me how that one memory was the one that stood out most over the course of their whole lives. Why? Why was that one thing so important to them? What would become the most important memory to me?

One January morning, I sat back in the pink cushioned chair of the nursing home, trying to piece together fragments of a particular person's life, when one man raised his hand. I stood up to sit by his desk, thinking he wanted help with some aspect of his story. This man had told me that back in the day, he was a bank robber. He said they used to call him "bat boy" in the papers because he was trying to save enough money to buy the Pittsburgh Pirates. (I checked the papers, and sure enough Bat Boy really existed at the time he said.)

"What are you working on?" I asked him as I sat down. I tugged my sweater away from my chest, sweating in the warmth of the nursing home heat. I looked at my friend, watching the skin of his cheeks sag as he spoke, causing his bones to stick out and his eyes to look bluer, like fragile glass.

"Rachael, trust me," he said, lifting a trembling, bony finger as he spoke. "Religion is the biggest cruelty mankind has ever seen, and one day, just like I did, you are going to find out it isn't true. Not a lick of it."

"Um," I responded. I looked at him. I looked at the clock to see how much time I had left. I wondered what to say.

This wasn't the first time my friend brought up religion with me. In fact, nearly every conversation had been in some way about his reconciling himself to, or apart from, religion. A self-proclaimed "bad Catholic," this man fell in love with Peggy, a girl he met in a grocery store in 1945. He said his heart jumped straight out of him and into her basket, and after she dragged him around for a while she threw that basket back on the counter and walked out of the store without a second glance.

He wasn't the first man to be struck like that by love. But when she left him, he prayed to the Virgin Mary. Unless Peggy came back to him, he promised, he would never marry. He wore this self-inflicted punishment on him all his life because Peggy never did come back, and when I met him, he said he was an eighty-four-year-old bachelor, shackled to his vow.

"Do you believe religion can ruin a man's life?" he asked me.

I crossed my legs and wondered again what to say. How much of a right did I have to speak into this man's life? "Maybe religion can ruin a life," I began, "but I don't think God as Creator is out to ruin the lives of the people He makes."

My friend the bank robber shook his head emphatically. "Just you wait," he said with confidence. "One day you'll ask questions you can't answer. Then you'll know what I know—there is no God."

I wondered for a moment, if he could *see* the pile of unknowns inside my heart, the anxieties, unanswered questions that have sat so long they're fermenting. I wondered if he'd believe me if I told him, *I have asked those questions.* That I may not have lost a Peggy, but I too have known grief and asked why. I too have sat in church and wondered if we weren't all part of a giant hoax. That I may never have taken bags of money from the vault of a bank but I too have regrets.

That I too have stayed up all night and longed for answers. I too have ignorantly wished for God to be nothing more than a well-wisher or a pleasant, elderly neighbor. I too have wanted to walk away.

I think part of the problem with the stigma of religion is that it's been put in the hands of people who wish to use it only to create power and order. People have used it for centuries to inflict guilt and shame upon others under the pretense of religion, when that has never been the message of the gospel. And we respond to it by wearing our guilt and taking lifelong vows to atone for ourselves somehow, changing God and tweaking the Bible until it fits our own preferences and comforts, or reducing God in our minds to something the size of a weatherman, whose only power could be changing our ten-day forecast.

I have asked and demanded a hundred questions of the Bible, of its validity and relevance. I have looked for holes, for inconsistencies, for historical discrepancies. But the Bible has stood up to every single one of my questions about its validity, leading me to believe that this Jesus is in fact the Son of God, that He is something more splendid and beautiful than we can even currently imagine, and He did not come to impose on us a series of rules and expectations we could never meet but rather to set us free from them.

I think Jesus, from what I've read and experienced of Him, would get along with my friend the bank robber as well as, and maybe even better than, the next person. I think He loves him, even after knowing everything he ever did, and died and lived again in order that he might taste life. And I wonder, in all those years in the church, if anyone ever told him that.

"Tell me you agree with me, Rachael," he said. "Tell me you don't believe any of this Christ business."

I agree with him that there are questions that don't have answers. I agree that religion has been used to manipulate and control people in a way Jesus never would. I agree that self-inflicted vows of punishment are not a good way to live a life.

But I cannot agree with him about this.

"I can't," I responded. "Because I do believe this Christ business very much."

The man shrugged his shoulders and threw his hands up into the air, like he was letting me go. "Well then," he said, "I hope it doesn't let you down."

Me too I want to say. Me too.

God's Promise: The Lord's Prayer

I think about my conversation with this man and wonder why we came to such different conclusions about faith. I wonder what it's done to each of us, what we are both left with.

Here are the questions I come back to again and again: Who is God? Is He good? Can I trust Him? What is His heart for all people? What is His heart for me?

I spoke with a friend of mine the other day about these questions, about why I am still asking them years down the road. She said there's a danger in answering anything too quickly, in thinking about something too little before we take a view on it. But isn't that what we see everywhere today? Instant opinions? Instant anger, instant retaliation? There is not much room for meditation in our culture. Maybe there has never been. Is that part of the reason why there is so much anxiety?

Think about when Jesus taught His disciples to pray. He tells them to address God as Our Father. This is done at the beginning of the prayer, before we ask for anything at all.

Maybe that is already a prayer.

I have not met any other two words that have soothed my own anxiety more. *Our Father.* First, to know that is the way Jesus told us to address God—not as sir, not as Master or Majesty, although He is all of these things. But most of all, He is a father. He is immeasurably big, gentle, and gracious enough to fill all the places where we are weak.

My earthly father is finitely gentle, kind, and generous. In the way of examples, I am inclined to think I've had the very best. It is not a stretch for me, when I address God as Father, to think of Him as involved, patient, compassionate, and soft-spoken, because these are all the things I have experienced of a father. Maybe it's because of my dad that Father is the easiest way for me to think of God, and the most comforting. When I think of God as Father I think, *maybe there is room enough and patience enough for all my questions.*

> Maybe there is room enough and patience enough for all my questions.

Secondly, He is ours. He is *our* Father. Therefore, *we* are not *I*, not one, not single or solitary. We are many, and He is ours.

There are so many things in this life that scare me because I think I am meant to face them alone. But if He is our Father, then we belong to Him; but we also belong to one another. We are meant to bear one another, pray for one another, love one another.

To share in one another's joys and sorrows is more than to be compassionate. It is to be ourselves, in our truest form, which is to become like Christ. We are communal beings, meant for continual fellowship. When we really care for our brothers and sisters, when we shoulder one another's burdens, maybe we are not simply being nice or good. Maybe we are simply taking hold of what we were created to be—a family.

This simple act, of reminding others, and being reminded myself, that we are not alone, is part of the difference between my life and the bank robber's. I owe so much of my understanding about God and how he might fit into my anxiety to people who have helped me see it. It is God-given grace to have people in your life willing to walk beside you. The people who have asked questions alongside me rather than trying to answer them for me, the people who have been able to sit with not knowing, the people who have told me it's okay to not have the answers, the people who have said, I know you cannot pray this right now so I will pray it for you, these people for me have been the church. They have taught me so much about the character and grace of God. They have reminded me we share the same Father. There is something in that set up that tells me God is good, that He calls us to care for one another, to be at peace, to pray, not to hate and not to let our opinions get in the way of our greater calling.

The Role of the Church

So where should the church be, in all this? How should the church stand with and support the inner workings of the heart? If the church is the body through which the kingdom of God is spread on earth, what role should it play in walking and sitting with the struggle?

It was church youth group, and I sat somewhere in the church basement among the pile of legs sprawled across grungy pink couches and green bean bags, probably wearing a mission trip T-shirt and athletic shorts. We had just finished our lesson, which I remember being very good. We divided into small groups to discuss and then eventually took prayer requests.

"I'd like to pray for my test on Thursday," one girl said.

"I'd like to pray for my mom. She has chemo tomorrow," said another.

We nodded solemnly. These were not good things, not exciting news, but they were tangible. We could pray for them. We could check them off a list and then follow up, ask with a smile, how did that test go? How was Monday's visit?

Another girl shifted uncomfortably. Finally, she said, "I am having a lot of doubt. I don't know if I believe in all of this. I don't know if I am a Christian."

Her request, so vulnerable, floated in the air for a minute, still whole, and then fell into our laps and broke like shards of glass. We looked around uncomfortably, each waiting for someone else to respond.

Finally, someone said, "I'll pray for you."

The problem was, prayer didn't fix it. Week after week, her doubts continued to grow, and we, her small Sunday prayer circle, felt ourselves getting annoyed. We'd meet her with trivia, with facts about whose bones were found where and when the earth was created. We'd read Bible verses to her about how the evidence of God was all around her, and it was a sin for her to not believe. We'd say, you just have to have faith.

It makes us uncomfortable, doesn't it? We don't like to hear that people are doubting, that any of this could be hard to believe. We can't fix doubt and uncertainty. They don't fit into a box we can tape up and track the shipping.

And deep down, I think we're all a little concerned because we have questions too.

In my experience, the church has been relatively silent on anxiety induced by doubt. There are thousands of conferences at churches in our country, year after year, about marriage, about God's calling, and about grief counseling. There are so few conferences and resources for Christians struggling with anxiety or doubt. The church often doesn't know how to handle the issue of the quiet doubts of the mind.

I think it's because the issue is complicated and invisible. They are quiet and suppressed, and usually there isn't an easy fix for them. Depression and anxiety can be lifelong struggles. I think we don't know what to say to people because we cannot offer them a formula. We carry around our own deep-seated insecurity that God might not be able to help, or maybe worse, that we won't be able to help.

In my experience, though, I don't need the church to offer me a formula. I need the church to have room for my questions.

Luke 24 records the story of two men who met Jesus on the road after He was raised from the dead, but they didn't know it was Him. Jesus asked them what they were talking about. They responded, "Are you the only one visiting Jerusalem who does not know the things that have happened there in these days?" (v. 18). They were disappointed. Jesus was not who they thought He was. These men shared the story of their leader, who was taken by the religious elite and put to death, and it was the third day. Where was He already? They wanted God to come—*now*—and fix things.

How often do we see ourselves in the same place?

Jesus knew the question they were asking. He could have answered it immediately and said, "Hello! Here I am, the Great Messiah, the one you've been waiting for!"

But He didn't because He knew there were other things they needed to understand. "And beginning with Moses and all the Prophets, he explained to them what was said in all the Scriptures concerning himself" (v. 27).

I am confident Christ could heal all our anxious hearts instantly, with the snap of a finger. He could wipe that fear from mind and memory, and I think for some people, He does work like that.

There are larger questions that must be answered.

It wasn't until later that night, after a whole afternoon of explaining the Old Testament, that Jesus prayed and the two men's eyes were opened. If Jesus had just revealed Himself to them immediately, they might never have understood the larger picture of why He came.

The Lord can use our questions and anxiety to make us ask questions we might not otherwise ask. If the Bible is really what it claims to be, then it will stand up to every test we put it to. The church, I think, is scared of the questions because the questions may take years to sort through, and they may make us realize our assumptions of who God is might be incorrect.

People with anxiety don't need to just "have more faith." If they could just do that, I'm sure they would. They need room to ask, to explore, to discover all the things they would never question if they never went down this road. They need people who are willing to sit with them and walk them through it.

If you know someone who struggles with anxiety, know this: they do not need your answers or your formulas. They need your presence and your prayers and your willingness to sit with them even when the questions are uncomfortable. They need you to not be silent.

Understanding My Sin

> Our Helper He, amid the flood
> Of mortal ills prevailing.
> For still our ancient foe
> Does seek to work us woe;
> His craft and power are great,
> And armed with cruel hate,
> On earth is not his equal.
>
> —Martin Luther,
> "A Mighty Fortress Is Our God" (1529),
> trans. Frederick H. Hedge (1852)

What is the relationship between anxiety and my sin? Is my anxiety a sin? Is it caused by sin? Are there specific sins in my life that fuel my anxiety?

We have such limited vision here on earth. We have a hard time seeing ourselves as we really are. There is a popular saying, "The devil loves to make people feel better than they really are or worse than they really are. Both are untrue, and both a form of pride."

Our world today doesn't like to see ourselves as we actually are. We like to see ourselves the way we want to be. Which way are you tempted? How do you tend to see yourself?

In general, I think people who experience anxiety seem to see themselves as worse than they are. Maybe it is because anxiety has shown them their inability to control themselves, calm themselves down, and think rationally. They know what it is like to be anchored to the bottom of the ocean, to be desperate for a breath.

Anxiety and depression are so closely related to each other, and often I think one can breed the other. In my own experience, I know I have felt as though there was something inherently wrong with me that I could not fix, and maybe God could not fix. I fear entering certain scenarios or conversations because of my anxiety, which makes me discouraged, and I start to feel worse about myself.

My anxiety, my questions, and my doubts, have pushed me to the Bible for truth. And while the Bible is about God, it has also shown me some clear truths about who I am.

The thing that is inherently wrong about me is my sin. Psalm 51:5 says, "Surely I was sinful at birth, sinful from the time my mother conceived me." Romans 3:23 says, "For all have sinned and fall short of the glory of God," and Romans 6:23 says, "The wages of sin is death." I don't have to look far to find sin in the world. We are broken people, wounded souls, capable of intense and terrible harm.

And yet there is something inherently right about me—that I am created in the image of God. I am "fearfully and wonderfully made" (Psalm 139:14). I am loved "with an everlasting love" (Jeremiah 31:3).

I am not unredeemable. I am called "out of darkness into his wonderful light" (1 Peter 2:9). In *The Meaning of Marriage*, pastor Tim Keller and his wife Kathy say, "The gospel is this: We are more sinful and flawed in ourselves than we ever dared believe, yet at the very same time we are more loved and accepted in Jesus Christ than we ever dared hope."

The hope of the gospel, for me, is that I can keep repeating these truths to myself. I can understand that, as a Christian, I don't need to live in fear. Christ loves me in my anxious state, and He calls me out of it. He reminds me through His truths what He has called me to. I repeat these things to myself daily, hourly, to remind myself of who I am in Him.

> Christ loves me in my anxious state, and He calls me out of it.

It is only through Jesus that there is hope for my pride and my anxiety. It is only through Jesus that I can see myself as I actually am, not better and not worse. It is only through Jesus that I understand that there is a real, physical weight to my sin, but also that He died to set me free from it.

Understanding Our Pride

Hannah's story in the first chapter of 1 Samuel has always gone straight to my heart. Hannah and Peninnah were both married to the same man, Elkanah. Peninnah had children, but Hannah did not. Elkanah loved Hannah, and while he provided for Peninnah and her children, he took extra measures in caring for Hannah. He brought her double portions of meat.

Peninnah was probably jealous. She was probably staring at Elkanah, watching him take special care of Hannah, watching him brush back the hair behind Hannah's ear as he looked at her for just a second longer than he ever looked at Peninnah. Maybe she froze in place, watching from the other room, one hand in mid-tousle on the head of a son, the other clenched in exasperation, thinking, *I gave you myself, and I gave you these children; am I still not enough?*

Through example, I think the Bible makes clear why polygamy is not a good idea.

Peninnah started wringing out her resentment and bitterness over Hannah's head. She clutched onto the thing she felt made her more of a woman than her rival: her children. She wore her badge of motherhood as proof she was more valuable than Hannah. Maybe she had decided that even though she couldn't make Elkanah look at her the same way, she could give him a namesake, and so that made her better. She poked and prodded at Hannah, reminding her that she could not do the one thing a woman in that culture was most valued for. She tried to irritate Hannah, to remind her she might have Elkanah's heart, but she could not have his son.

Hannah went up to the Temple weeping. She prayed so hard, "in her heart," that Eli the priest thought that she was drunk (v. 13). She asked boldly for the Lord to give her the impossible: a son. In exchange, she would give her son back to the Lord for service.

It's hard today, when a woman has the power and opportunity to do so many things, when motherhood has become a part of her but not the whole of her, to imagine what it must have felt like to be a barren woman then. Hannah, though, understood something maybe only her infertility could have shown her: that God provides all things, and a life is given at His hand, rather than a person's will or volition. She recognized that truth and asked for a son, offering to give him back to whom he rightfully belonged.

Peninnah, in her resentment, paraded her children in front of Hannah to boost her own pride. Hannah, understanding all things, even Peninnah's children, come not from Peninnah but from God, humbled herself before the Lord. When the Lord gave her a son, she named him Samuel, which means "heard by God."

Anxiety is a double-edged sword because it rises out of a need to control what we cannot control. Ultimately, though we try, we cannot control when we live or die, what will happen to those we love, what people will think of us, how we will find our dream job or dream spouse at the right time. We cannot control these things, and so we are anxious, because at least that is taking some kind of action. Like Peninnah, we believe these things will come from our own efforts, if only we try just a little bit harder. How many of us are anxious because we seek security? And isn't that what Peninnah wanted too? The security of being loved?

First Peter 5:7 tells us, "Cast all your anxieties on him because he cares for you." The verse directly before that reads, "Humble yourselves, therefore, under God's mighty hand, that he may lift you up in due time."

They seem like a strange pairing of verses. What could humility and anxiety possibly have to do with each other? Humility, here, leads to being exalted. God is close to the humble. I think Peninnah's arms must have been so tired from lifting herself up, scrapping for that place at the top because life is better there. Maybe she could only tolerate herself at a higher altitude. Don't we all like ourselves more when the air's a little thinner?

Hannah was completely humbled before the Lord. She could have been anxious every month, waiting to see if finally she had done the thing she so hoped to do—conceive a son. Maybe it took being barren for Hannah to depend so completely on God, to realize she had nothing outside of Him, but she did.

To be humble and to be at peace, even when everything seems wrong, are both counterintuitive. But because He cares for us, we can be humble—it is God who provides, not our own efforts. Because we are humble, we can accept His care; we can be honest about what falls like sand between our fingers. Both, together, are water from a deeper well than we will ever reach by our own digging.

Advent: The Gift

It is mid-October, and my whole life is the swell of my belly, so big my husband Andrew's shirts are a crop top on me, so big that getting out of bed some mornings is an insurmountable challenge, so instead I sit in bed and have tea brought to me and use that giant belly as a shelf, and I think, *today, baby June.* Today would be a good day to come. The day we have been waiting for, marked with a circle and several exclamation marks on the calendar has finally come, risen into full bloom, so that the leaves outside our window burn against the sun, and when we open the windows we smell the crunch of the leaves and the smoke of yard fire.

But June doesn't come, not today or tomorrow or the next day. I find myself overdue, overcooked, waiting, still waiting. I am hesitant to make plans because of the inconsistent contractions, the headaches, the fact that I have approximately zero shoes that still fit over my ankles.

I am no longer *just* waiting for this baby: my life is wrapped in the complete and circular suspense. The wait has wrapped itself around me until this impending event and myself can no longer be separated.

There is nothing I can think about, nothing I can do, until you come. I am tied up completely in the advent of you.

> Now the Earth was formless and empty, darkness was over the surface of the deep, and the Spirit of God was hovering over the waters.
>
> —Genesis 1:2

God incarnate entered the world through a pregnant woman. I wonder if there could be a more beautiful, accurate way to show the world His anticipation, the swelling, the bursting to come forth into humanity He was about to redeem than in those final days, when Mary was swollen with expectancy and hope, so physically in the moment she was unable to think about anything else.

God hovering. Doesn't that also sound like a pregnancy? A pregnant woman hovers over her body, counting contractions, paying attention to all the signs, to every twinge and pull, ready to bring forth something new, fresh, and marvelous. Is that the way God looked at the world He was going to create? Is He rubbing his hands together? Is He laughing? Is He consumed with the life and beauty He is about to bring forth?

"Let there be light." These are first recorded words of God we have, which are found in Genesis 1:3. I've thought for a long time about the significance of those first words. In the throes of my anxiety and my questions, my doubts about how a good God could permit evil, about whether He hears me, about why or if He loves me, when I cannot shed my anxiety—these first words have been an anchor.

We know from the first words that the Bible is primarily a book about God: "In the beginning *God* created the heavens and the earth" (Genesis 1:1, emphasis added). In the beginning, *God created.* In the beginning, *God.* There is nothing in all creation, made or unmade, that has not been held. And this is a mystery I don't understand, a mystery my mind is not sharp or full enough to see clearly, and so I can only grasp at the smoke around the edges of it and see that it says, *in the beginning God.*

What we are, where we live, the air we breathe, the organs and blood cells that make us up as people, that is all created by God. All our thoughts, our emotions, our hopes, dreams, feelings, were once held in the hands that created it all.

We learn from this first statement who the Bible is about. For too many years I have read the Bible as a book about myself, a personal life script, designed to tell me what to say and what not to say, what to think and what not to think. And in some ways, that is the natural reaction to reading it. But this first sentence tells us who the whole Bible is about. It is about God. God, who is all encompassing, all fulfilling, whose existence was never called into question. God, with the ability to create out of sheer will, who simply breathed and spoke, and the whole world was created, this world that has taken us thousands of lifetimes to explore and begin to understand. God, unlike the other creation myths in the ancient Near East who spoke of gods that triumphed over beasts, disorder, and then created order, simply called the world into being, to order. He simply stirred the cosmos and brought forth life. God, who created every heart that has ever beat, every lung that has ever breathed, every eye that has ever seen. God, who created you. God, who created me.

So the Bible is about God. It is about His brilliance, His glory, His character, His love. It is about His mercy, His justice, His compassion, His redemption. And in order to ever understand ourselves or this world we live in, we must first read the Bible as a book about God. Only then can I begin to think *that* is why this world is so big and so unattainable, why the universe is beyond my comprehension, why my emotions and my fears feel so much bigger than me. I did not create them, any of them. I can only understand all of this from the point of the created.

And the first thing He created was *light*.

Why light? By light we see and we understand, know, comprehend. By light we see and live. So here is God, at the beginning of time and space and everything else, about to birth creation.

Don't you hear that same excitement in the first chapter of John? "In the beginning was the Word, and the Word was with God, and the Word was God. He was with God in the beginning" (vv.1–2).

Did God know, and did Jesus know, in the beginning, the plan for the world's redemption? "In him was life, and that life was the light of all mankind. . . . The true light that gives light to everyone was coming into the world" (vv. 4, 9).

With the anticipation, expectation, of a woman in full bloom, God gives the world the light He has been foreshadowing throughout all history.

After thirty impossible hours they place my baby on my chest. When I think about my daughter, who I carried inside me for nine months, about the nausea and the hip pain and the exhaustion at the end, and then about the baby that was born, I think about how the first thing I asked when she was put on my chest was *where did you come from?*

What was the correlation between the way I watched my belly grow and the baby who was now placed on my chest? What had I done to grow an arm, a leg, a stomach, a brain? I never felt closer to the heart of creation than I did that first moment I held her in my arms. I was a witness to it. I felt, holding that baby, like I could feel God, when He created man in His image, saying it was *good*. Look at this thing that happened to me. Look at this soul I harbored. Look at this darling, fearfully, wonderfully made, whose heart I can hear, whose hands I can touch. Look at what God has done. And this is the way I was made as well.

My body, finally, had burst with the anticipation, and here was the realized hope. Here was my daughter, with her very own beating heart.

Here was every hope, every expectation for this child in tangible form.

> The next day John saw Jesus coming toward him and said, "Look, the Lamb of God, who takes away the sin of the world! This is the one I meant when I said, 'A man who comes after me has surpassed me because he was before me.'"
>
> —John 1:29–30

Why did Jesus come that first time? According to John the Baptist, it was to take away the sin of the world. The Angel Gabriel told Mary she would give birth to a son who "will be great and will be called the Son of the Most High. . . . He will reign over Jacob's descendants forever; his kingdom will never end" (Luke 1:32–33).

Did Jesus take away the sin of the world? Every day, people, young and old, die from murder and sickness, marriages shipwreck, and people steal and lie. My daughter, praise God, has not yet discovered the world can be a scary place, but what will I tell her when she finds out? That the world has just always sailed along with an undercurrent of sorrow, and that's just the way it is? What if she is like me, and I find her one day strapping to her back questions too big for her, questions I cannot save her from the weight of because I cannot answer them myself?

Emmanuel came, God incarnate, the light that is the only true light, into a place that still is so very dark, and I wonder, *Jesus, why didn't You just finish it then?* Yet I know already You do not work on our timelines or according to our own expectations.

If I think about it, the way my children are born is not the way I would choose to grow them. I would wish to think them into being, to have the thought and then the child, without any of the pain, or the waiting, or the slow quiet growth. I would want for them to sleep through the night immediately, to not *need* me so much, to just be aware of where they begin and end and to know their boundaries. I think the same things of myself—I don't want to walk through the years of incomplete understanding. I don't want to question, I don't want to be puzzled. I want *knowledge* of the world; I want to be able to see things as they really are.

My baby and I are both slow-growing processes. And I wait in expectation of them both. Though I cannot see it now, that must be a beautiful thing.

The world waited for the Messiah with great expectation and longing. They waited and watched and finally when Jesus came it was in the quietest, most unassuming way. Why didn't He just sweep through and save everyone? Why did He come so quietly? Why did He make His coming so easy to miss, and yet, those He touched were inescapably changed?

God values the things we overlook: the quiet, the hidden, the ordinary. He came into the world through a woman's damaged reputation, and He died a criminal's death. And all those days in between He ate and drank and *lived* with people. He built with His hands and He walked with his feet and He attended weddings and dinner parties. He came not to impress the rich but to minister to the poor and the sick. So what does that all mean for this daily, extraordinary life we live? What does it mean that Jesus gave so much value over to the *process* of being born, of living, of having relationships, of eating, of working, that to redeem humanity He didn't swoop in and pull us all out? He entered in and lived *every minute of His life.* He enjoyed the creation He made. He loved the people He made. He lived completely in the wait, with a body that could and did fail Him, and He lived in perfect peace.

What does that mean for my life?

I live in advent of a lot of things. I am always waiting. I wait for a baby. I wait for that baby to sleep through the night. I wait for a new kitchen. I wait for a vacation. I wait for a baby who will talk to me. I wait for a realized career. I wait to stop being anxious. I wait for spring.

Jesus waited years, uncountable years, from the beginning of creation until He came. And then, when He came, He lived for years in the brokenness around Him. And He healed some of it, He died for all of it, and He rose again to defeat it, but we still live in the shadow of brokenness. We live in hope, but we still live in the wait. So there must be something about the waiting that is holy.

In His ministry, Jesus fed five thousand people, people who followed Him and waited because of His miraculous signs, and this was an overwhelming miraculous sign: Jesus has the power, the will, and the resources to feed all the hungry who follow Him. But everyone who was fed still became hungry again eventually. They weren't cured of hunger forever. They were still completely human.

Jesus also demonstrated immense compassion and power in His ability to heal the sick. He was unafraid of the leper, and He brought back to life dead children. But He didn't heal everyone. He didn't storm the leper colonies and cure every person in sight. He didn't take every person who had been bleeding and stop it. And everyone He did heal eventually died of something else. He didn't make the physical healing or the hunger quenching permanent.

Why didn't He?

I can only guess the healing He came to do must have been far deeper than the physical self. I can only imagine the physical healing done by Jesus during his time on earth was the smallest glimpse of the healing He died to complete in every heart.

But there must be something in the wait—because we are still waiting for Jesus to come again. We still experience loss, sickness, death, tragedy, hunger, despair. We still live daily in the dichotomy between the saving grace of the gospel and the reality of sin still present in our lives.

The longer I am a Christian, the more aware I am of the condition of the world, as well as the natural condition of my heart. The more aware I am of sin's hardness and pervasiveness. I have more questions and fewer answers. I live sometimes under paralyzing anxiety, like Wendell Berry said in *Peace of the Wild Things*, over what my life and my children's lives will be.

I am also, however, more aware of the hope. And every day I live in a broken body and a broken world, hope of the eternal becomes more precious to me.

So what does it mean?

And God said, "Let there be light," and there was light.

And the light came into the world.

And by that light, like C. S. Lewis said, we see everything else.

And that light lives in us.

Maybe we cannot know hope unless we know sorrow. Maybe we cannot know hope realized unless we know hope awaited.

Maybe this whole life is like a second pregnancy, and as we deal with the aches and the sickness, we are promised hope fulfilled. Maybe Jesus' way of working in us is every bit as unassuming and surprising as His life. Maybe it is the most seemingly ordinary moments that are precious ground for change and understanding. Maybe, when I look back on my life, it will be the hardest parts, the waiting parts, the ordinary parts that will be most important to me, because that was the steady work of Jesus on my heart. And at that time, maybe I'll finally know what He was making me into—I'll finally understand fully what it is to be made in His image.

I live today in the wait of my second baby. Halfway through my pregnancy, I fill my days with coloring, with the park, the swings, the pool, with pickles and cheese, with "Mama, go" and nap times and endless amounts of laundry. I fill my days with counting kicks and imagining another nursery, with playdates and tiny shoes and finger smudges across the wall, with cravings for fruit pies and hip pain as I fall asleep. I think, *there is so much in this life I can't wait to show you, baby. There is so much we will read and talk about. You'll learn the smell of cookies baking, the burning orange our tree turns in the fall, the cool water of the creek at the park by our house. There is so much joy waiting for you.* Advent is expectation of light.

CHAPTER 3

When I'm Anxious about My Marriage

We stood at the altar, hands clasped together, twisting rings onto shaking fingers. I had to point you to my left hand so you would get the ring on the right finger; do you remember that? We smiled so big I thought we'd break, and with trembling lips we spilled out vows repeated by couples just like us for centuries. We promised ourselves, each to the other, and I hoped to give you the world. You were about to become something new, my husband, and neither of us knew yet what that would mean for us, but you had the same eyes you've always had, the same ones I fell in love with, and I thought, *it's still Andrew under there. It's just only and completely Andrew.*

What is it that draws people to each other? And what is it inside us that makes us want to spend our lives with another person? For me, it was Andrew's kindness. He is an old soul, and I think that's why people are drawn to him. Even in college he liked to wear his slippers, read the paper in the morning, and drink his coffee black, and to me he's always seemed to possess more years than the number assigned him. Andrew's a listener, one of those rare people who never need to announce their own value or accomplishments to a room, maybe because he just *knows* them inherently, and if I ever lose him at a party, I know I will find him in a corner, nodding and listening to another life story he always seems to invite.

I was twenty-two years old when I walked down that aisle. At the time, it felt like I had waited months, maybe years, too long to become Andrew's wife. I felt grown up and in love and like I already had enough life under my belt. After all, I had been legally allowed to drink for a full year, had lived in another state, and had probably learned all there was to learn about love and life. Andrew and I said those vows to each other while our hands shook and we tried not to cry, and all those people we loved stood around us with cameras and big smiles. I think both of us were so sure on that day, so desperate to be sure, that we would love each other forever. We thought, *here is something new and beautiful. In this relationship we will love and listen to each other, and we'll never hurt each other. This is our new forever.*

When I think about those early days of marriage, I think what surprised me most was the fear. I couldn't have expected that on our wedding day because it was sunny and warm, a blur of fancy dresses, hair spray and new shoes, of peonies, handshakes and hugs of friends and family who had traveled across the world to celebrate us, lemon cake, toasts, dancing. So many times that day Andrew and I looked at each other with that overwhelmed happiness, two introverts who wanted to sit and absorb and process every event of the day. When two people are in love, it is usually only for themselves, but on a wedding day, their love turns inside out for everyone else to see, maybe for the first time. They share the intimacy, the commitment, the desire to forever be joined with one another with everyone else they love. It's a vulnerable day, but a beautiful day when the people who love them and care for them also decide to stand around them. Maybe it's like the flame of one candle spreading across a thousand wicks, until all you can see is the light.

We wanted to be so big, Andrew and I, like meteors soaring across the sky. We wanted to be adventurers, to be air and light for each other. That day it wasn't hard to believe marriage would make each of us everything for the other.

What I remember from those early days is the way we danced around each other as we set up furniture, asked each other what we wanted for breakfast, decided which side of the closet would be ours. I remember the first time we had new friends over for dessert— not friends who knew us before we were Andrew-and-Rachael but friends we met as a *married couple*. I remember moving the dishes from here to there, and then back again, agonizing over which angle we should have the table at. We were trying so hard to be grown up and figured out, and I think we were scared we wouldn't pull it off. I think we were each trying not to show the other that we both wanted to go back home to the way we grew up, to the place where things were comfortable.

I pictured my marriage from out of a catalog, a daydream made sweeter by the distance between us that year of engagement. I pictured spending our mornings making chocolate chip pancakes, strolling through farmer's markets hand in hand, spending afternoons hiking, reading, or trying new restaurants. What I didn't picture was the two of us being human. I didn't picture needing to manage a budget, the financial implications of him starting his own business a month before our marriage began, or wrestling through what it actually meant to be a man and a woman in a marriage and how to live as image bearers in those roles. I didn't picture dealing with my sin or my husband's sin or wrestling with the anxiety I couldn't run from as a wife. We walked into our marriage as barely more than children, with no idea how much we had to learn. We thought love had been conquered already by us. And maybe that was grace: agreeing to carry one another before we knew what we'd be walking through.

The Gift of Marriage: A Partner through the Questions

We had a whirlwind first week as husband and wife, driving nineteen hours, unpacking our things and repacking for our honeymoon. Three flights and twenty-three granola bars later, we walked along the beach, soaking in the warm June humidity, sweat and salt sticking to our skin. We walked and walked, until the world grew dark around us, and we watched the moon come up and listened to the waves slap on the sand, and I tried to walk faster, to out walk the waves and the moon and everything that was bigger than me. The world, before my eyes, felt suddenly far too big. I couldn't understand my existence. I couldn't understand why I was there, what the point was of marriage, why other lives turned out so differently from mine. I breathed heavier, told Andrew I was dizzy, and sat on a rock while I pulled back my hair with my hands. I was having a panic attack, but I didn't know how to admit that at the time to myself and especially to Andrew, who had no idea how anxious the year I just walked out of had made me.

The year before, living in Raleigh, I experienced death, brokenheartedness, sorrow, grief, and fear more closely than I ever had, and I walked into my marriage with a broken theology and shaky faith, not knowing yet that it would be months, years, of trying to pick up the broken pieces of what I believed and put it back together. My honeymoon was the first time I slowed down in a year. Everything I had been through hit me like a powerful wave, and I panicked.

Andrew had married a person working through a train wreck. If he didn't know it before the wedding, he found it out on the first day of his honeymoon. I was, for lack of any better description, *so* afraid. I had experienced my first taste of grief the previous year. I had no idea what I was going to do with my life, and I was grappling with huge questions about God—if my life mattered and what I was supposed to make of the world around me.

If he regretted his decision suddenly, if he wished he could turn around and change his mind, Andrew didn't show it. Andrew sat down next to me on the rock, and he didn't say anything. He just reached out and took my hand, and we watched the waves come into the sand. I teetered at the brink of falling off the edge of the earth, and his hand became the anchor that kept me there.

Andrew never once tried to answer my questions for me. He never acted like I was being overdramatic, or emotional, or crazy. Had he done that, I don't know that I would have ever explored the validity of my anxiety the way I have. Andrew sat with me, through it all, just like he did that first night. Our first year of marriage was the year God let me fall into every one of my questions. I felt unprotected. I had a crisis of faith as I watched several people in my life die of terrible disease, all while I tried to manage a new home, find a job, and navigate a new town. But I also had Andrew to make me cups of tea every morning, to hold my hand and pray aloud for me on the nights when panic of not knowing felt as though it would crush me, and to listen without judgment while I said things about God, about myself, about him, that clearly demonstrated how confused, hurt, and afraid I was that year. I look back on that year and think it was when I had Andrew that God let me fall. It was Andrew, through his patience, acceptance, and ability to listen, who helped me finally work my way back to God. It was Andrew who helped me see God was really with me through it all.

I wanted to be the perfect wife on my wedding day. What bride doesn't? What bride doesn't think she will never say anything negative about her husband, or disappoint him, or allow him to frustrate her? What bride doesn't think she will have the marriage that is flawless, a perfect row of beautiful photographs where she is laughing and young and still in love in every single one?

On my honeymoon, I realized I would not have that perfect marriage because I myself was so broken. I needed a lot of help facing everything in my heart. I was so worried I would disappoint Andrew, that I would not be everything he dreamed I would be. Maybe we would fall out of love. Maybe we married the wrong person, or maybe we just married each other too young.

But Andrew helped me see the point of marriage isn't to fulfill a prescribed role for the other person. Marriage is about being *in it* with one another. Marriage is about walking the other person through every high and low and reminding them that the one who holds it all holds them. Marriage is about encouraging one another, pointing out the way God is working in the other, praying for the other when they can't pray themselves.

That first year of our married life was the first year I felt the full weight of the anxiety, doubts, and fears that had been building up inside me for most of my life. But it was also the first year I wasn't alone—and that was a great gift.

Andrew does not think the way I do. He does not ask the same questions, carry the same doubts, worry about the same things, or fear the same ends. We believe in the same God, and yet our faith has taken us on such different routes. Andrew and I have read the same books, and enough of our lives have been lived next to each other at this point that we share most of the same experiences. A book that can be profoundly comforting and helpful to him is disconcerting and stressful for me because it talks about an issue he can take at face value and I cannot. This is helpful because it allows me to see that not everyone is like me, and it allows him to see that not everyone is like him. And he has been an anchor for me, in many times of doubt and anxiety, because I know his faith and personal life very well, and I can see firsthand the fruit in his life.

For example, a topic Andrew and I know equal amounts about— that is to say, not very much in the grand scheme of things—but have different reactions to is the subject of heaven and hell. We have both read about it, and we both understand it. Andrew has no problem believing there is a hell because of what he knows about people and the way they are drawn to sin. I have a very hard time reconciling the belief that there is a hell because of what I know about people and the way they are formed in the image of God. At some point we both have to take the Bible at its unfailing word, and it is immensely helpful to do this alongside someone who has the same faith as me, who is exceedingly kind, and who does not question the same way I do. Andrew listens to every last one of my questions and doubts, and he never tries to convince me I am wrong or crazy; he just sits and says he is glad not everyone thinks like him. My wonderings never bring him down; they never cause him to doubt. And that is a comfort and a gift to me, to have a safe place where I can talk things through, start to finish, without interruption.

> Maybe the gift and the work of marriage are tied in with each other. Maybe the gift is in the work.

Maybe the gift and the work of marriage are tied in with each other. Maybe the gift *is* in the work. Maybe we get anxious about our marriages because we want them to be perfect and easy, rather than a reflection of the way Christ loves his church. Maybe we want to be two whole, complete planets orbiting around each other, never needing to intersect. If this is our hope for a marriage we will only be let down because it means either we do not know each other or we have not let ourselves be known.

God's Promises for Our Marriages

My marriage was not everything I dreamed it would be those weeks leading up to my wedding. Praise God for that. I wanted lazy mornings and long vacations; I wanted zero hard days and no challenges. I dreamt of Andrew and I being faultless, knowing instinctively how to love one another perfectly. Instead, it was through our flaws that Andrew and I found out who each other really were, and both of us found out what it felt like to be loved through that. We discovered, and are still discovering, the joy and confidence that grows out of knowing you are loved, exactly the way you are, knowing your spouse will do everything in their power to bring you closer to God.

Shouldn't that be the culmination of any marriage—to recognize the hope of the gospel is that people can change because God changes us? Shouldn't it be about two people who over time have uncovered everything that is broken in the other and lifted them up to the only One who can make it whole? To learn to hold it and surrender their brokenness and not use it for manipulation and revenge? Is there anything more vulnerable, more beautiful, and in the end, more powerful to the testament of the grace of Jesus? It is a beautiful thing when two people can remind one another that God is not finished with us yet, that He who began a good work in us will carry it forth to completion until the day of Christ Jesus.

I think Andrew and I would both say one of the greatest gifts we've experienced together happened the year we decided to read through the Bible together. We just looked at each other one day and realized that for as long as we'd been Christians, neither of us had read the Bible the whole way through. We thought it was something we should probably do, so we decided we would. We had no idea at the time how much change it would bring to our lives.

We started when our baby was about two months old, in that time when you can leave infants on tables or counters and they will just lie there without moving and sometimes just put themselves back to sleep. Every morning, after we finished breakfast, we put our baby down, refilled our coffee cups, and listened to our reading on audio. The words of the Bible filled our kitchen and seemed to change our hearts so quickly and permanently that we could almost *see* it happening. We learned that year about God's heart for the broken, the lost, the unsure, the faithless, all of which we were. That Word spoken aloud in our kitchen seemed to fill the chasms in our souls we didn't know we had.

When we read that book, something changed in the way I looked at Andrew and at myself. I began to look at him with the reverence and awe that comes with realizing the person you know best is a deliberate, intentional work of creation. Through reading the Bible, I began to really learn and know that my husband was crafted and put together by the hand of God. And so am I. None of that is conditional on what we say or do but it surely *changes* what we say and do. We're learning what it is God calls us.

We became lighter that year, even with a house and a baby. I think there's something about knowing, through and through, that you're forgiven that is wholly freeing. It means there is nothing in your life you have to hide from yourself or your spouse because grace covers it all.

Andrew is still broken, and I am as well, and we are like two icebergs that sometimes collide and chip each other more, but we realize now that it is not the brokenness that will define us or this marriage. It is the grace that covers it. And maybe our only job as husband and wife is to be patient with one another and be the voice that will remind the other, *God is not finished with you yet.* Yes, this is hard; but this is not the final you. In all things Christ has supremacy, and He will one day have supremacy in you.

Maybe marriage is as delicate and as full of strength as the wing of a butterfly: rub or bend it the wrong way and it disintegrates, but give it air and room and it will carry something twice its weight a great distance. Maybe marriage is like flashes of lightning—intense moments of vibrant joy nourished by the kind, steady reminders each day that we are both works in progress. Maybe marriage is taking all my anxiety and insecurity and asking why it's there, asking what kind of gift it might be, what it might teach me about the way I am loved. Maybe marriage is two people holding hands silently by the fire in a moment that will never be Instagrammed or recorded or shared with anyone else. It's just a steady reminder to each other that I see you as you are, and I love you anyway and always. Maybe it's learning to see one another through the smoke.

These are the promises from God I have learned to hold to in my marriage: God is not finished with me.

A Picture of Grace

What are a husband and a wife supposed to be for each other? What are they supposed to expect from one another? What makes a marriage real?

I think the answer must be different for every couple. Marriages are as diverse as human souls, as widespread and as unique, filled with different interests, hopes, longings, and desires.

I've encountered a lot of anxiety in the marriages of people I love as they try to sort out one another's roles. There is anxiety around where that person fits, who should be doing what, and what it means to glorify God in a marriage. I think to a small extent, these questions are normal and healthy. It's good to think about what your marriage means and how it should be lived out.

In our premarital counseling, Andrew and I were told that the man should take out the trash and do the budget, and the woman should keep the house. We have not found this idea to be based on anything written in the Bible, and Andrew and I do not follow it. Most of the time, I take out the trash, we both manage the budget, and Andrew, a fabulous chef, helps a lot in the kitchen.

The question I have found to be most important in our marriage is this: How does what I am doing bring good things to my spouse? That means I have to look at myself and ask, Am I encouraging? Am I being honest? Am I praying for him? Am I a tangible picture of the grace extended to my husband through Christ?

I think the kindest way we can care for one another as husband and wife is to not expect so much of the other that we forget to see them, and not to expect so much of ourselves that we become anxious or guilty of what we are offering. I think what serves our spouses best is to consider what ways we can see our spouses not only for all they are but for all they one day will be.

We get thousands, maybe tens of thousands, of days with our spouse. That's a lot of time for a person to evolve, change, and grow. The privilege of marriage is that we get to walk with them; we get to witness part of what they will become.

CHAPTER 4

When I'm Anxious about Motherhood

The clock read 6:04 a.m., but I only noticed the florescent lights, sterile gowns, and lumpy hospital bed. After endless hours of labor I had forgotten everything but that moment. As I lay on a bed strapped to machines, the epidural blissfully numbing my body, as I threw water bottles at Andrew telling him *wake up wake up please, it's time,* and then just deciding to push the call button and carry on without him, so he woke up from a dead sleep to a room full of people and wondering why he was soaking wet. *Somewhere in my life I got a master's degree,* I think. *I traveled to Guatemala by myself for a summer and survived. I used to think about homemade croissants and television shows and talk to people about literature.*

All of that was another world far away from that dimension I was sucked into where it is never day or night, only pushing, Pitocin, florescent lights, and a baby that will. Not. Budge.

After an eternity of pushing, suddenly she is here, and they place my nine-pound-seven-ounce mountain of a baby on my chest, and I am cuddling her and asking for water, so much water that I will need a catheter in a few hours to expel the three liters of fluid that built up in my bladder. I think, *I carried you, baby, I carried you and now you're here,* and in my arms is the most intimate stranger I have ever met, a human I grew but do not know. How will I take care of her body and soul when I don't even know her name?

This was my initiation to the world of motherhood. The next welcoming came that night, when my exhausted body was woken every two to three hours to feed her again. It was the first of many, many nights—awake when the rest of the world fell asleep.

I don't like to be awake when the rest of the world is covered under the nest and shadow of the dark, tucked into blankets, heads imprinted on pillows, warm bodies pressed together in the most perfect peace of the day. When I wake I feel as though I am cheating, like I am seeing a part of life and the world that no one is meant to see. There must be a reason our bodies need to shut out the world and consciousness for a third of the day.

When I lie there, in the dark, I can feel the worries my body knows to instinctively let go of while I sleep begin to pile up again. They flutter around me, fold themselves over me, and I feel like I need to sift through each one before I can surrender again to the lull of the night. That's when the questions come, that's when I worry about the future, about the past, and about my soul and the souls of people I love. I think that's when the questions are the sharpest, because there is no light to break them up. Why would God create someone to send them to destruction? Did I say the wrong thing to that person today? Who have I hurt this week? How are we supposed to forgive when we are hurt? My daughter is growing. How is she growing? What will she become? What will all of us become? Can we trust a God who created darkness?

The early stage of motherhood was a blur of three-hour sleep cycles, of never having enough and also having abundantly more than I could have imagined. Does any new mother ever get enough sleep? It was frustration, fury, wonder, and awe in the same breath for this baby I grew but did not yet know. And the nights—the nights had moments of peace, holding that little hand as my baby nursed and fell back to sleep, but mostly, the nights were a strange mix of extreme loneliness and wanting to be alone in my own bed, not awake with pressing worries and wonders and a colicky baby who cried against the quiet of the dark. I paced the floorboards of my house feeling like I was being swayed by the questions, the insecurities, the fear of the unknown, the love I tried desperately to cultivate.

Psalm 63:6 says, "On my bed I remember you; I think of you through the watches of the night." Did David hear this from a mother? As I rocked my baby through the hallways, both wanting sleep and afraid of it, because I knew it would catapult me through time, into the future I could not control or predict, I began to think that maybe, if I could just blow these worries to the side a little bit, on the waves I would see the God who is not linear.

Meditating on these truths, I was finally able to see this wakefulness as something of a gift. I held my baby close, and through her cries, I rocked her and lifted up my own griefs to God. When she was inconsolable, I bounced and nursed and cast my own anxieties and fears on the God who cares for me (1 Peter 5:7). I took every worry about my own inability as a mother to love and protect my child and lifted them, each waking hour, to the God who taught us to address Him as Father. I believe, looking back at those nights, that my baby and I were tucked safely into the love of the everlasting arms. Maybe God gave me and every mother this worry and wakefulness to teach us to meditate. Maybe, without it, I would never have come to love the verses in the rich thin pages of my Bible.

Maybe God gives mothers wakefulness and worry to teach us to surrender and to mediate. Maybe He wakes us up again and again through the night to remind us that He cares for us, that He takes care of and gently leads those who have young. Maybe He's giving us time, in the quiet of the night, to sift through our fears and hand them back to Him, to let Him rock us as we rock our babies, to teach us that we are vessels. Maybe He allows us to watch our husbands and other children sleep in perfect peace because it's a small taste of whole, complete peace to come. Maybe all of this is designed to make us love Him more.

> Maybe all of this is designed to make us love Him more.

Maybe one day I'll find out that that among other things, the wakefulness was the greatest treasure I could have been given. The wakefulness was really the gift of time.

What We Were Created For

One thing I have learned so far about mothering in these years with little children is the worry that accompanies mothering is anything but little. Those first days with my baby June, I asked things like, "Why won't she stop crying?" "Why doesn't my baby like me?" "Has she filled enough diapers today?" and always, "How do I make her go to sleep?"

As the months progressed, questions began to center less around *does my baby like me* and more about *why is she pulling on her ears, is her cough as bad as it sounds,* and *when should I call the doctor?* I spent so much, too much, of that time on Google—so many midnight hours when I should have been sleeping were instead spent staring into the white florescent of the screen as I scrolled for answers to my questions in a thousand forums. If I have gleaned one ounce of wisdom from my twenty-two months of mothering thus far, it is this: Google is never your friend at two o'clock in the morning. There are always approximately 2.5 million answers to any question you have, all conflicting, and none of them will make you feel better in the moment.

But all of these little questions and little anxieties about how much our babies are eating or sleeping and why they are crying reflect a set of much deeper, harder-to-answer questions that I think most mothers are asking. We obsess over nap time, over baby-led verses parent-led feeding, over sleep training. But don't all of these questions, at the heart of them, ask the same thing? Can we keep our babies safe? Can we give them what they need? Can we love them well?

The first time I found out I was pregnant I stood in the soon-to-be nursery of our new home—the one without doors, with half-sanded floors and painted walls. I stared at the test and, like any new mother, thought it could not be real; I tried to find the connection between the two pink lines and the eternal soul inside my body. How does a soul form? Is it one piece at a time, like the cells of a body? Or is it whole from the moment of conception, a complete, eternal person? Or does it come together in a way entirely different from that?

It's a blueberry, the doctors told me, when we went to our first appointment. Our blueberry grew into a lemon, into a peach, into a grapefruit, into a watermelon. Why do they use fruit to describe what a baby becomes? Have you ever watched a fruit or vegetable grow in a garden? Little baby watermelon that grow and ripen until they are ready to pick? They grow from little to big, but they also are already a fully made watermelon in miniature form. This is a mystery to me. My baby did not grow from a blueberry to a watermelon, but a *baby*, little to big, a whole, complete, baby.

Head shoulders knees and toes, eneey-meeney-miney-moe ran through my head over and over as I watched two little legs kick their way across a black screen. The head, the tiny little webbed hands, the heartbeat that was not mine but lived inside of me, going up-down-up-down, blinking like a strobe light.

Andrew told me later that he never wanted to forget that moment—holding my hand while I lay on the table in an oversized hospital gown, tears streaming down my face as I watched this little life move and wiggle in front of me—that he wants to trap it in a jar and watch it, revisit it, as many times as he needs to be reminded that this is what *life* looks like, in its earliest beginnings. That at the beginning of it all, the heart starts beating, and our hearts break and swell and crack as we watch that one on the screen because it is, for the first time, not mine or his but *ours*.

On the screen I watched the curve of a little round button nose, a tiny tummy and a head that was building and constructing the brain my baby would one day think, reason, and love with. The midwife told me all the major organs—the kidneys, the intestines, the liver—are already in place, and now all the baby has to do is grow and expand and be nurtured. I heard the heartbeat—the strong, steady sound of life, the heart that would carry this baby through this pregnancy, childhood, through life and love, this little heartbeat that represented the beginning of it all and the fullness of what this baby will become. And this was happening *inside* my body. I have never been more sure than I was in that moment that this is *exactly* what I was created for, just what I was meant to do.

So there is something to this—to my baby being kept safe without my acknowledgement, without my conscious effort, without my understanding. I worried so much, those first months of pregnancy, about what would happen to the other soul inside my body if that heart I watched on the screen stopped beating. I wondered a lot about the word *miscarriage* and the blame it places on the mother. If I miscarried, does that mean I did it wrong? And what can be done right, when it is all done in our subconscious? In a strange way, it was a comfort to me, during those months, to not have any idea what it takes to build a placenta or a kidney or a lung. My body *did it* without my consent or consult, the way it breathes without my permission, and I think that is a grace, that we aren't the ones who decide what happens next.

I began to think a little then about the concept of carrying my baby home. We spent weeks preparing that nursery, from the bunting to the pink walls to the Winnie-the-Pooh framed pictures my mother-in-law gave me. We washed baby clothes in Dreft and dreamt for months about carrying our baby home, about giving her a bath, about putting her to bed inside that floral room. And I began to think about God's disposition toward my baby. Did He love her the way I would grow to love her? Could anyone? And what did it mean if something happened to her in the womb; what will it mean if something happens to her in life? Jesus loves the little children, and I realized that on my part, it would all come down to trust in the end. I had to trust that if God can form a soul and form a body part, then He can also take care of it. And my job was to carry this baby and to trust that if God loved my baby, then no matter what happened, I would carry this baby home, to this life or the next.

God as Creator and Keeper

This brings me to maybe the most real questions about motherhood: is my baby's soul safe? What will she grow up to be? Why, of all the people, all the places and eras in history, is my life here, linked to hers? Will that have an impact on who we are, eternally? Why, of all the mother-daughter pairs in all of time, are June and I paired together? What is it that we'll learn from each other?

In those early days, when June would get fussy or upset, I used to hold her to my chest, *shhh* in her ear, and rock her until that neck, getting stronger but still so loosely controlled, finally relaxed into my shoulder. She would breathe out as I breathed in, the two of us an accordion, unfolding into one another's notes. I think I knew, even then, that she was growing: that it would not always be appropriate to comfort her in that way. Already she is too big to hold for long around my second growing bump, and I know the day is coming when I will not be able to rock her until her worries melt away. She won't remember those days of rocking, so I think maybe I did it then to rock her in advance. Maybe it was for all the storms she will go through one day—maybe, without being aware of it, I was trying to assure her in all the physical ways so that when she is too big for it, she will know still, instinctively, that she is loved.

In motherhood I have learned this: the veil between *here and there,* now and eternity, is very thin. June was not, and then she was, and what had I to do with that? She kicked and grew inside of me for nine short months, and then out of me came an eternal soul, sewn up and packaged into a tiny, temporary body that will one day expire, but *June,* my darling girl inside her skin never, ever will. And isn't that something? To watch that tongue learn words and her brain comprehend and know that *here* is someone wholly immortal?

Andrew and I read a wonderful book by Sally Lloyd-Jones in those early days called *Thoughts to Make Your Heart Sing.* There is a section of the book that stands out to me so poignantly. It is about birthdays. For Christians, there are three—the day we are born, the day we become a Christian, the day Jesus carries us through death and into life forever. I think about where June came from, the place where she was intimately knit and sewn up, and it doesn't seem so very far from this world. It is my fervent prayer and hopeful joy that June will know this in her heart, but ultimately I cannot make this decision for her. Isn't that the hardest part about motherhood? To trust the God who created our babies with their souls? Will Jesus carry my babies home?

I understand it is neither within my duty nor my ability to bring my child into salvation. As a pastor and family friend said to me once, "Some parents watch their children become Christians and think they had something to do with it." Salvation is the Lord's, maybe like creation is the Lord's, and we can witness and partner and rejoice in it, but we are not responsible for it. I have wrestled with this, I have fought against this, and I think I am finally starting to understand that this too is a grace. God knows my babies far better than I do, physically, emotionally, spiritually, and I must, at the end of the day, trust Him with that.

Does God love my children? Will He take care of them? Today June and I drove with the windows down, and she laughed, kicked her legs, and shouted, "Breeze!" the whole way to our destination. Every now and then, I reached my hand back, and she grasped it tightly and swung it back and forth, saying "Mama, Mama," and I thought, *this is joy.* Here is something good and pure. And if every good and perfect gift is from above, then this shows me God cares for me and for my daughter. Whatever else, I can hold to that.

So what is my responsibility to my child? I think it is only, and completely, for her to know that I love Jesus and to be transparent about the way the grace of the gospel has shaped my life. My job is, thank goodness, not to love her perfectly or even make sure she eats perfectly or sleeps perfectly. My job is to point her to the one who *is* perfect in all things, who promises to make all things, my children's hearts included, new. My job is to pray for them, to trust in the everlasting arms more than I trust Google or baby books or mom blogs, to rejoice in His mercies made new every morning, to see the gift I've been given in the family I love so much.

> So what is my responsibility to my child? I think it is only, and completely, for her to know that I love Jesus.

Growing Babies in a Fallen World

Part of the weight and the questions I've experienced in motherhood is that I am getting more of a glimpse of my own sin—how big and pervasive it is and how it affects every area of my life.

I can't think of anything quite like strapping myself to the verbal, adamant, half-formed logic of a toddler day after day to bring out in me my own impatience, my selfishness, my desire for comfort—which in my heart equates to solitude, silence, and a hot cup of tea. After nearly two years of motherhood, I am seeing, and believe I will see even more closely with another baby, my own short temperedness. I very often stop thinking about the eternal work that needs to be done in my child's soul and start thinking about the immediate thing that needs to happen so I can get some quiet.

The curse bears weight not only in that we give birth to our children in pain but that we experience the pain of raising them in a fallen world. In birthing June, I expose her to sickness, to hurt, to disappointment, to grief, to loss, to wrath, and to neglect. There are so many ways in which I am tempted to worry for her life and safety, and I'm sure those ways will grow as she grows.

We also bear the weight of knowing we parent imperfectly. This reality has been a cause of great anxiety for me. In some way, during June's life, I will inadvertently cause her harm. I could be the cause of her needing to go to counseling one day. I carry so much influence over the way she will first learn to think about herself. I want those to only be happy, positive ways, but I am fallen. I am incapable of giving her that. I can only give her hope.

What are God's promises for us in motherhood? What can we hold to, when there is so much darkness? Scripture tells us, "He tends his flock like a shepherd: He gathers the lambs in his arms and carries them close to his heart; he gently leads those that have young" (Isaiah 40:11).

I watch my daughter express genuine joy, excitement, and kindness, and I think, *where did that come from?* Did I teach her that? Or is it God, who is holding her in His arms? Is it God, gently leading me, when I call to Him from behind this blindfold of my sin? What is God stitching together inside of her?

I grew up in the outskirts of Buffalo, New York, where the winters are brutal but the summers beautiful, a breath of two months that stretch out like one long sunny day. It's a crime, up there in that house I was raised in, to be inside in the summertime—to give away a single moment of sunshine before the clouds reappear in the fall.

We didn't have air conditioning in our house—it seemed like a waste when you have only a few months to enjoy the warmth, so instead we threw open the windows and let our bare feet stick to the hardwood floor. When we visit now, as adults, we stand at the counter on the hottest days, chopping up cucumbers, berries, and lemons for the perfect afternoon refreshments. We arrange snacks onto floral trays: mixed nuts, French bread, and smelly cheese. We carry everything out in trays onto the lawn, where that five o'clock hour casts a golden glow on the table we moved to the grass. We sit down to enjoy our drink and nibbles, to bask in the golden glow, to converse with each other.

It is afternoons like this that make me most aware of the passage of time and makes me long for the day where time stands still, the conversation lasts forever, the sun stays right where it is, as we listen to the mourning dove and watch the fireflies slowly light up around us as the night descends. It is these afternoons that make me wonder what heaven will be like.

Why would we have moments and days like that if there wasn't a God and if He wasn't good? Why would we have pleasures like good food and loud laughter, the prickle of sunshine on the face, the carbonated fizziness of our drinks dancing in our stomachs, engaging, challenging conversation, humor, memory? It is these days, I think, that I most profoundly experienced grace in my life. It is these days I have felt most held.

So what does this say about God with us in motherhood, despite my sin? What does it say that my parents, who were imperfect, also managed to cultivate relationships among their children so that they look forward to days and conversations like that? What does it mean that I also long to give those to June?

God, be gracious. God, be enough for our faults. God, save our children.

It is all a prayer, a lesson in understanding love.

CHAPTER 5

When I'm Anxious about My Calling

When I was thirteen years old I became friends with a war veteran named Marty. Marty came to our Sunday school class one morning to talk about his experience in World War II. I didn't understand then the kind of bravery it would take to open up to a group of middle schoolers about the hardest and most formative years of your life, years you would spend the rest of your days trying to reconcile and make peace with. Marty talked to us about fighting, about following orders from our country to kill, to destroy, to conquer. He talked to us about his uniform, about eating dinners from a can, about waiting for letters to arrive, about hoping he would live long enough until the next shipment arrived. Marty cried while he talked to us and tried to explain the weight war has on a person for a lifetime afterward.

As a thirteen-year-old who had never before talked in this much detail to a war veteran, I was so moved by his willingness to share his story with us. I wrote Marty a thank you note, and he told me in church a few Sundays later it meant a great deal to him because he had gone home that day and berated himself for crying in front of us—real men didn't cry. We became fast friends over the summer, and when Marty moved to Oregon in the fall, we continued to write to each other for the next ten years.

Marty and I were an odd pair to become friends: he a hero, a veteran, a scholar, and me a teenage girl with braces and no idea how she was going to fit into the world she was growing up into. It was through letters to Marty that I first discovered my mind processes more clearly through writing than speaking. Marty was one of the first people who told me I should consider writing as a career. "You need to keep writing, Rachael," he used to say in his letters. "You are already a writer; you need to keep writing."

I brushed it off and told him I couldn't write, not really. There was no career in it for me. At fifteen or sixteen, I was already experiencing a great deal of anxiety over what I was supposed to do with my life. None of the careers that came up in my personality tests at school—teacher, counselor, director—seemed especially appealing to me. Secretly, I *desperately* wanted to write for a living. I had half-written novels tucked under my bed and filed away on my computer, but I thought it was a selfish, unstable career—not meaningful or sure enough.

The anxiety around what to do with my life continued as I finished high school and started college. I changed my major three or four times, always staying away from anything English or writing-related because I thought I couldn't do it. What I learned in college is that people of our generation are desperate to do something meaningful with their lives—to have a career that helps people and makes a difference in the world. Our careers are a huge aspect of our lives—and we've started to think they are the largest way we will contribute to society.

One would think that for Christians, this anxiety would be lessened—that we would recognize the work has been done on our behalf, that our greatest calling is to love God and then love our neighbors, but I see almost *more* anxiety around the subject of calling in the Christian world. We put pressure on ourselves to somehow discern what God wants us to do with our lives and then immediately find a job that fulfills that calling. Our fear is that we will not only let ourselves down, but we will let God down. If we choose the wrong career, we will no longer be living God's best for us. We will somehow be outside of His best will for our lives.

Even if we know enough about the Bible to know it's bad theology to believe we can mess up God's plan, don't we still feel it a little when we're making important decisions? I know in college, though I wrote constantly in my free time and loved to read almost more than anything, I felt as though my career had to be *helping* someone, and if I wasn't doing something like starting my own school in a remote country of the world, it would be less than God's best for me.

I traveled to Guatemala on a teaching internship between my sophomore and junior year of college. While I traveled the impoverished countryside, taking photos for a slideshow to present back home, it suddenly occurred to me that wrestling with calling is a privilege. So many people in this life and world don't have the space or room to think about what kind of career they are going to have. They are just trying to survive. So was I missing something in Scripture, in my Christian walk, by *agonizing* so much over this decision?

> Wrestling with calling is a privilege.

One morning a few weeks before I got married, I sat on a bench by my favorite lake. Journal and pen in hand, I was taking the morning to think about what I was going to do with myself after I got married. What kind of job should I look for? What was I *supposed* to do with my life?

So as I sat with my notebook and brainstormed ideas, I watched the ducks waddle in and out of the shallow water in front of my bench. It occurred to me that ducks didn't worry in the least bit about their calling: they are ducks. They fly, they mate, they raise babies, they swim, they collect food. It doesn't seem like they carry too much anxiety around with them about what they are going to do with their lives.

I wrote to Marty during this time. I told him I was about to get married. He couldn't come to the wedding because by that time he was in his mid-nineties and had some health issues. I told him about the question of what to *do* with my life. "Write, Rachael," he said without hesitation. "You need to write."

I told Andrew about the letter, flippantly, casually, like I didn't really care what Marty said or what he thought about my career.

"Do you like to write?" Andrew asked me. I was about to marry this man, and he knew only a little about the hidden novels, of the character sketches, of the huge tub of journals in my childhood closet.

"Yes," I choked out, trying not to cry, wondering what was so significant, so meaningful about admitting this.

"Then try that," Andrew said, like it was so obvious, like this was what I was supposed to be doing all along.

"I can't," I tried to explain. I wasn't properly trained. I had missed the chance to study it at college. A pastor told me once that I should wait for a call from God regarding my vocation, and I had received no such thing in the area of writing. Plus, it didn't feel like a noble career or one that would really help anyone but myself. It seemed a selfish way to live, indulging every day in the thing that brought me joy.

Andrew asked me if I loved writing, and I had to admit that I did. I found few things as beneficial to my personal life, as relaxing, as difficult, and as satisfying. "Well," he said, "I think God wants us to do the things we love."

I stared at him. Was it really that simple? Did God just want me to do the thing that brought me joy, no strings attached? Was it a worthwhile career if it wasn't feeding people or physically saving them, if it meant long hours in solitude, without investing in meaningful relationship?

I answer that question today with a wholehearted, resounding *yes,* but at twenty-two there were too many other factors in my life to answer that question clearly. It took years of wrestling with that question, reading biblical books on calling, and studying God's Word to finally answer that question.

What is God's will? What does He want us to do with our lives? Do our careers matter to him? How do we know we're in the right place?

The year I graduated from college, my dad, brother, and I traveled to England for my cousin's wedding. We spent a week together visiting family and celebrating my cousin and his new wife. The wedding was in the same part of the country where my mom and dad went to school, met, first lived together, and where my dad became a Christian. My husband's family is from the town he and I live in now, and I marvel every time we pass his grandfather's childhood home, just a few blocks away from our own. For me, to see my mom and dad's first apartment was an emotional, rare experience. I knew I would likely never see it again—but this was where they started. This was where they began their rhythms. This is where they understood each other.

A thousand stories from my dad's memory came to the surface that week. It seemed every corner we passed, every old brick building, had some kind of significance. *There is the place we went on our first date together! You mom, an island girl, didn't know how she would sit in the car for forty straight minutes. There's the house we stayed in, right before we moved to America. It was freezing—no roof, so we woke up with frost on the sheets, but you wouldn't believe how friendly our hosts were.*

Sunday morning came round and we went with my dad to Above Bar Church in Southampton—the place where my dad became a Christian. He was a doctorate student in electrochemistry at the time and had no interest in Christianity. He wanted to go to a concert that night, but his friend said he would only go to the concert if he came to church with him first, so my dad went. That night he became a Christian. Thirty years later, we stood next to my dad thinking, *this is the place.* This is the place where the Hound of Heaven reached him, and in a way, reached us all.

So this was a calling, in a sense of the word. During this trip, which we later called *The Pilgrimage,* I saw maybe more clearly than I ever had what God wanted for my dad's life—which would be the same for what God wanted for my life. My dad chose chemistry. He chose his university. He chose his program.

God chose him.

God used my dad's love of chemistry, essentially, to bring my dad to Him. When my dad started his doctorate program, one of the six candidates were Christians. By the end, five Christians graduated. I think they all discovered in that time a higher calling than their vocational one.

What does God really want for our lives? I think it is to know Him and to love Him. What are the two commandments God gives us? We are to love God and love our neighbor. In the Bible, when He wants something very specific done of a person, He doesn't play tricks on them or make them guess what it is He's asking of them. When He wanted Abraham to move, He told him. When He wanted Esther to become queen, He sent Mordecai. When He wanted Joseph to marry Mary, He told him.

I am not saying we should throw away the idea of vocational calling. It is clear we are all different people, gifted in certain ways and provided different opportunities. I am saying that maybe we've got it upside down when we are paralyzed by the idea of calling. Maybe it's when we are unable to focus on our larger calling of who we are called to *become* and instead focused on what we are called to *do* that we need to reorient our idea of this word.

Here are the ways God calls us:

> As a prisoner for the Lord, then, I urge you to live a life worthy of the *calling* you have received. Be completely humble and gentle; be patient, bearing with one another in love. Make every effort to keep the unity of the Spirit through the bond of peace.
>
> —Ephesians 4:1–3 (emphasis added)

> But you are a chosen people, a royal priesthood, a holy nation, God's special possession, that you may declare the praises of him who called you out of darkness into his wonderful light.
>
> —1 Peter 2:9

> I pray that the eyes of your heart may be enlightened
> in order that you may know the hope to which he has
> called you, the riches of his glorious inheritance in his
> holy people, and his incomparably great power for us
> who believe.
>
> —Ephesians 1:18–19

Calling, then, is always done in a positive light. It places more emphasis on the work God has done and is doing on our behalf. It is not unclear; it is not anxiety inducing. We are always called into assurance, into light, and into hope. We are called *away* from guilt and fear. Choosing a vocation should never be done with anxiety, with stress, with duty, or with guilt.

Pastor and writer Kevin DeYoung puts the idea of calling this way in his article, "What Is My Calling? (And Is That Even a Good Question?)" for The Gospel Coalition:

> In short, if this is what is meant by "calling"—know yourself, listen to others, find where you are needed—then, by all means, let's try to discern our callings. But if "calling" involves waiting for promptings, listening for still small voices, and attaching divine authority to our vocational decisions, then we'd be better off dropping the language altogether (except as its used in the Bible) and labor less mysteriously to help each other grow in wisdom.

I decided that summer after I married Andrew that maybe I would try writing after all. I started a blog. I started doing freelance work for interior paint companies and county bureaus. I checked books out from the library and began a terrible novel about the Civil War in Virginia. People kept asking me to write, began hiring me for projects. I loved it. And I found that it was through writing that I seemed to work out my redemption. Writing became an avenue by which I could process and respond to what I read in the Bible.

So maybe writing was a calling for me. Or maybe teaching, or waitressing, or counseling would have worked out just as well. It is through writing that I have been faced with the depths of myself, that I have begun to see how much I am in need of a Savior. Writing has helped me see in a better light my true calling.

When making a career decision, we should ask ourselves, do we want to do this? Are others asking us to do this? Is there opportunity to do this? But we should not presume to think that, if we are praying about our decision, we will make the wrong one and therefore have to live God's plan B for our lives. God is far bigger than our decisions. We can be at peace knowing we are in his hands.

> God is far bigger than our decisions.

My brother is a cellist—and he is good at what he does. When he plays the cello, it sounds like the world holds its breath, like all of life is on pause for those moments his music fills the air. And when he finishes, that last note hangs in the air. It makes everyone listening look up, think about where the music came from, where it went. That, in a way, is a calling—like looking up from the sand to see the ocean for the first time, like finally grasping how expansive the sky is. Maybe his music is a duet, or maybe it is an echo, of the place where music never ends, where there is no final note. It stirs every heart listening, the curtain call, the thought that if creation could give us a gift like music, that alludes to something about the Creator that calls every one of us.

CHAPTER 6

When I'm Anxious about My Friendships

I didn't expect my college roommate to become my best friend. In fact, I anticipated the opposite.

I met her by accident a few months before our freshman year began at one of those orientation days where students walk around with their parents and try to act like they aren't nervous at all. I was desperate to make a good impression. I smiled and said hi to everyone I met thinking that if I could just *show* everyone I was three steps past friendly, I would be able to survive my first year away from home.

Enter Alana.

We both started college as elementary education majors, so we were in a few sessions together that orientation day. I passed Alana in the hallway on the way to lunch. It was just the two of us in the hallway. No other students, no other commotion or distractions. I thought, "Here is my chance to make a friend," and stopped as she passed. I waved and said hi. Alana looked directly at me, then straight ahead, and continued walking—*without saying anything*.

I was shocked. Here I was, literally putting myself out there, showing her how friendly I was, how approachable, how aware, and she *walked right past me*. I took note of the name on her tag and thought, "I will stay away from that girl."

You can imagine my disappointment a few weeks later when I received a letter with Alana's name as my roommate assignment.

I found out later that Alana had no recollection of this story. She says she never saw me. And she became one of the greatest gifts to me in those four years of college.

You go to college to get a degree, to start a career, to move on with your life. But it was college, and my friendship with Alana, that did so much to transform my life.

Alana and I had the same major, and were both middle children, second girls, and people pleasers—we wanted to be understood. We loved each other from the (rocky) start. It wasn't long before we were doing everything together. We had so many of the same interests, hopes, dreams, and desires. I felt as though our lives were a constant repeat of *you too?*

Alana quickly became my best friend at school. We went night rollerblading together, we ate almost every meal together, we made other friends together. We talked for hours at the library when we were supposed to be studying, and then we went for runs together. We spent breaks at one another's houses and went on vacation together. She was the first person, in a lot of ways, who really got me. College is where I earned a degree, where I learned to live on my own, where I met my husband, but before all that, it was where I met Alana—whose loyalty and consistency taught me so much about what it is to be a friend.

What Is the Correlation between Anxiety and Loneliness?

In an age where we have everything at our fingertips—information, food, comfort, education, opportunity, and entertainment—our society seems lonelier than it has ever been. In fact, one common Google query in the United States is *how do I stop being lonely?*

We use Band-Aids like busyness and social media to cover it up, to shout loudly about how *un*lonely we are. We avoid relationships, we avoid conversation, slowness, all because we do not have the time or attention span, and then we wonder why we are lonely.

Loneliness directly contributes to anxiety. We are not creatures who are meant to live alone. There is a depth and richness of life we are made to experience: long talks around the dinner table, company and the warmth of a fire, hearty laughs and experiences shared with one another. When we lose true connection with other people because we are too busy, we retreat into ourselves and stop seeing clearly. We begin to live in the dark—and then start to think there is something wrong with us, something unknowable. Anxiety increases because things like that always increase in the dark.

Are you lonely? Am I lonely? I have been. Somedays I am still. Lonely of what? What is a human being? What are we made for?

All of us come into this world by way of another. We are put into being by an act of two people coming together, and then we grow within our mothers until we can breathe on our own. Our mothers grow us; our mothers are with us every second while we develop the essential things in life: heartbeats, circulation, breath, movement. And then, when we are born, we are helpless. We need to be cared for every minute. We need to have physical needs met, as well as emotional ones. The evidence supporting the importance of touch, interaction, and care in a baby's development is astounding.

We are made not only for ourselves. We are made for God's enjoyment and the enjoyment of others. I mean this in the purest sense of the word, the way a mother coos at and celebrates each milestone her baby makes, while caring for and meeting every one of those demanding needs in the thick of it. We are made for interaction, for meaningful connection, for *delight*. And when we have too much isolation and solitude or too much superficial interaction without anything real attached, I think maybe we begin to lose sight of who we are.

What is it in our time and place that makes life lonely? I think all of us know the answers to that. But how do we make friends? How do we learn to develop and sustain friendships that are sincere, honest, and trustworthy?

Do we believe we are worth befriending? Maybe that's the question we should begin with when we struggle with anxiety and loneliness. Do we believe we are still inherently valuable, creatures worthy of knowing and loving, beautiful, unique, and with so much to offer?

Everyone has a desire to connect with someone else, to love and to be loved. And I think all of us, on some level and for some reason, believe we are unlovable. People who experience anxiety or depression often experience a level of shame. And that is why reaching out to people and being loved in that vulnerable time is one of the truest pictures of grace and of our own redemption.

Hope for the Anxious Heart: You Are Enough

Maybe when it comes to making friends we worry we are not enough. We live in a society that thrives on comparison, and it is all too easy to fall into the comparison trap. This is a trap we can never win.

What happens when we compare ourselves to others? We begin to set our own schemas for success and value outside of God's standard of what is valuable. We begin to think we need to become more like some other person rather than like Christ, and by doing so we step into darkness. We begin to think there is not enough wholeness or abundance to go around. If a friend has accomplished something, like running a marathon, we suddenly think, because we have not accomplished that specific thing, we are a little less whole—that their wholeness somehow equates to us being less than. One person's accomplishment is all we need to confirm our own detriment.

The plain old truth is none of us is enough, and all of us are enough. We will never be enough because we are sinful, paradoxical creatures, prone to saying one thing and doing another. We are selfish, we are manipulative, we are determined to show only one side of ourselves. And yet, we are completely enough. We are redeemed, we are inherently valuable, we are created in the image of God with purpose and beauty and the ability to love.

> The plain old truth is none of us is enough, and all of us are enough.

We compare ourselves because we want to fit in. And we want to fit in to whatever definition of success we have created for ourselves. We all want desperately to identify as *in,* whatever our own *in* might be. We think if we could just take the tangible steps required of us, we will finally attain that long sought after *belonging.*

This past year, I have learned so much about the art of listening well. I'm in a dinner club with three amazing ladies. Once a month, the host picks the main dish, and we all bring sides: enchiladas with guacamole and tortilla chips, loaded potatoes with bacon, cheese, and sour cream, and always, always, decaf French-pressed coffee and dark chocolate for dessert. The host of these dinners also picks a question and sends it out in advance: What are you celebrating? What are you proud of? Where are you growing?

After dinner, we press our coffee and move into the living room where we pile up on sofas and tuck blankets around our waists. One by one, we answer the question. There are two unspoken rules. First, no answer is wrong or bad or invaluable. Second, no interrupting until that person is *completely* finished speaking.

It's hard for me to put into words how incredibly awkward, and incredibly healing, dinner club has been for me. I am usually the question asker. I am an internal processor and usually collect my thoughts by writing. I rarely share what is most pressing on my heart because I don't trust the other person to listen and I don't want to impose on their time. To have as many straight minutes as I could possibly want just to *talk* about *myself* with three thoughtful, insightful women ready to listen and eventually, when I'm finished, ask further questions, was incredibly out of my comfort zone. The first time I shared, about what I was proud of, I think my answer was a total of thirty seconds. But gradually, over time, I began to really open up with these women. And trust is built when you realize no one is going to interrupt you or finish your sentence for you. I realized they were giving me space to be me, to connect with me, and to affirm, in this way, that what I felt, thought, and shared was *enough*.

Talking with these women allowed me to process my doubt and anxiety in a way I hadn't been able to before. I was able to speak freely, without worrying what they would think, to understand where it came from, to pull the silver threads of truth I could hold on to through it all. By listening to me well, they offered me a form of friendship and belonging that is meaningful and life giving. They also offered me a friendship where I realized each of us could experience abundance in Christ. One person's success does not come at the expense of the other. There is not a need for comparison between us. We are all walking out our own journeys.

> Greater love has no one than this: to lay down one's life for one's friends.
>
> —John 15:13

Is this the way Jesus loves us? Is this the way He allows us to be ourselves, the way He tells us He has covered all the ways we are not enough so that in Him we finally can be? Is this the way he listens to and cares for us?

Maybe the type of friendship and connection we need in this world is one that offers people space and freedom to be themselves. Maybe we need to offer grace when we encounter others as themselves in every way. Maybe then we could really love people rather than worry about being enough for them, because we already know we *are* enough, we've found the place, the only place, where every need is met, where we finally are enough.

Friend, may you know, deep down, that you are *enough*—in your job, in your church, in your friendships, in yourself. You are deeply loved by the only one who was ever enough, and at the foot of the Cross, you have been made whole. Anxiety does not make you less than in your friendships. Rather, your anxiety can be an asset in all of your relationships. By it we can increase our empathy, understanding, and grace for others. By it we can understand the patience of the God who never gives up on us and in turn extend that patience with others. By our anxiety we can see we are loved completely anyway, and we can extend that unconditional love to our friends.

Don't let the lies win or the darkness and loneliness keep you from being real. State it boldly and confidently.

You are *enough*.

What God Says about Community

Community is not just a benefit of the Christian life; it is necessary for it to function. Hebrews 3:13 says, "Encourage one another *daily*, as long as it is called '*Today*,' so that none of you may be hardened by sin's deceitfulness" (emphasis added).

We tend to convince ourselves we are supposed to live out so much of our lives and faith on our own. In the spirit of freedom, of independence, of bootlegging it, we think we are supposed to wade through the deep waters of struggle, question, and fear on our own. But don't we call God *ours*?

Andrew and I have dear friends who are also fabulous travel companions and wonderful cooks. We love to spend time with them. We spent a weekend in their beautifully restored 1930s condo in Pittsburgh a few months back, and I spent some time talking about my own fears as a mother. My friend looked at me, after listening very carefully, and said, "I think part of the hope of the gospel is that you aren't meant to work through this on your own. That's what God gives us other believers for."

> Part of the hope of the gospel is that you aren't meant to work through this on your own. That's what God gives us other believers for.

My friend was right. Even motherhood, the job that was *only mine* for my specific child, was not something I should face or do alone.

It is through community that we start to understand ourselves: what we are, what we aren't, what we are created to become.

How to Befriend an Anxious Heart

One of the common misconceptions about anxiety is that we can fix it, that we need to fix it, or that we are able to fix it. This is why I think so many people with anxiety are afraid to talk: we are afraid other people will try to fix us and then walk away when they realize they can't.

Anxiety is complex, deep-rooted, and different for everyone, but I have found there is no easy fix for it. It can present itself in a thousand different ways and change its look in every season. Things that bring us no anxiety one year can paralyze us the next. There is no rhyme or reason.

The most important thing we can do when befriending someone with anxiety is to be gentle. Don't assume you understand their specific struggle. Give them space to breathe, give them quiet to think, give them a soft space to land.

My friend Jayna is, in so many ways, the very opposite of me. She is a businesswoman, an entrepreneur, one of those women who is just going places. She'll be on the moon the day it opens for business. She is an achiever and an extrovert, the type of person who can go to another party every night and not get tired. And yet, she is one of the most hospitable, space-giving people I know. She has not asked questions the way I have, and she has not wrestled the same way, but she has given me space to do so in our friendship. She has listened to me, without interrupting, and she has never made me feel like I am someone in need of fixing. She has allowed my questions to linger, sometimes for years, and is always willing to go back to them. Because of the space and the intentionality she gives me, her friendship is one I treasure.

My younger sister is a hospice social worker. She spends her day with the dying, and I can't think of anyone more empathetic or better suited for a job like that. One of the things she tells me, though, is that at the end of their life, people don't want to be alone. They want someone with them. Isn't that a testament to one of the deepest needs of the human spirit?

I truly think the best way to honest, life giving, deep friendship is to be the first person to ask the question and the last person to answer it. Don't assume you know what the person across the table is thinking. Allow yourself to be surprised by them. And, though it's so natural and easy to think we need to know the answers, it might be more valuable not to—to sit and listen, sometimes for years. We must let one another know that we are not alone.

CHAPTER 7

When Social Media Makes Me Anxious

What makes us anxious?

Sometimes I think the answer can be found in the fact that our skin changes color in the sun.

We are creatures made for light. For the majority of us, we work during the day and sleep at night. Our rhythms naturally change depending on the season. In the summer, we stay outside later. We take picnic dinners of tomato and basil sandwiches down to the creek and get ice cream at the general store. We sit out on Adirondack chairs around the fire and talk until the fireflies look like offshoots of the flames. In the winter, when those nights come early and stretch long, we cocoon inside our homes. We make stews with truffle and slow-cooked beef, we cuddle up by the fire, and we sleep for longer.

Today, there are many other sources of light. And I wonder if that is what makes us anxious.

The phone sits in front of me, silent, not ringing, its sleek, hard body not sweating like I do in the sticky air, the summer sun. And still, I wonder why I am anxious.

It is what can only be described as a *June day*, those perfect hours of early summer when the air is humid but not unbearably so, when flowers bloom strong and tall, the sky turns a piercing blue, and a gentle breeze, strong enough to ruffle my pages but not turn them over, tickles my hair and my skin.

I have an hour. A whole, circular, sixty minutes for no one but me and the pen and the paper. I should be scribbling madly. I should be soaking every single one of these seconds that the clock ticks, because we all know that complete hours for just ourselves are so few.

All I can think about, though, is the back of that phone only inches from my hand on the painted blue table, this phone that does not breath, laugh, or need to eat like I do, that will not move from its place, inches from my hand, unless I pick it up and move it myself. This phone occupies the contents of my mind.

Maybe I missed his call, I think. Maybe she emailed me back.

Across from me, down the three steps of my porch, on the other side of the sidewalk where my basil plant droops lazily over the rim of its pot, the beginning of tiny flowers are budding between green leaves.

It has taken me ten minutes to notice these flowers, just a little farther away from my phone. *What else have I missed?*

The telegraph was invented by Samuel Morse in the 1830s and 40s. Lines were constructed between great cities across the country so that even Maine and Texas could communicate.

Henry David Thoreau pointed out in his book *Walden* that Maine and Texas might have nothing to say to one another.

Everything now, is fast. Food and Internet and traveling and telephones and growing up. It is all there, instantly, so quickly that I wonder if the earth has had to turn faster to compensate.

Author and poet Wendell Berry once said he doesn't believe in using screens. And maybe he's right. They are, after all, artificial, giving off a light that neither warms nor burns the skin. They only make our eyes sting until, finally, we look up to rub them with a squint, as though we cannot believe the world is still there, this world outside that has become secondary to our screens.

We can use this screen, now, to track what the sun will do in the sky, the motion of the stars at night, when the spray of the tide will be highest. At nighttime, rather than embrace the dark, we fight it with lamps and dull the activity of the brain with television. When we walk, we look not into the light of the eye but into the slow, addictive light of our phone that reaches up and around us like a black vine, numbing our minds while whispering steadily, *you need me, you need me.*

We have exchanged real light for artificial. And we wonder why we are anxious.

Why do we even like social media? Why are we drawn to this other, two dimensional, filtered version of ourselves and other people? This online version of peering through the windows at our neighbors—what is so appealing about it?

I think what is attractive about social media, especially for people drawn to intellect, is that it is easy. It is so easy to scroll, to read casual life updates. It is like scrolling through *People* magazine. We see what people had for dinner, we see their baby's first tooth, we see beaches, vacation photos. We see each person as the star of their own life.

I love *People* magazine as much as the next person. It feels like a treat for me to sit down and see what the celebrities are wearing and where they are vacationing. But it is not substantial. As a magazine, I think I understand that. I know it is not bread for my mind; I know it will not stretch me in any way. It is easy.

Facebook, Instagram, Snapchat, Twitter . . . Is the problem not so much that we have these accounts but in the way that we use them?

Are we starting to use them as our bread and butter? Do we find ourselves going to these sites any time we feel the urge to check out or take a break? Is it the proximity to our phones that makes it harder to set this boundary?

I wonder about the way social media changes the way we view others and ourselves. I have seen some really good things come out of it. I have been able to watch people share their opinions, interests, and voice in a way that is hard for them in real life. I personally have been able to reconnect with people I would have lost touch with a long time ago. Social media can be fun, positive, and encouraging.

Social media, though, also has a negative aspect to it. I think it breeds comparison and reinforces the idea that we are only worth what our peers think of us. I don't know that it makes us think, as we scroll, about what it means that each person we come across is an image bearer of God.

In Philippians 4:8, Paul encourages us with this exhortation, "Finally, brothers and sisters, whatever is true, whatever is noble, whatever is right, whatever is pure, whatever is lovely, whatever is admirable—if anything is excellent or praiseworthy—think about such things."

Do our social media accounts challenge us to think about what is noble, right, pure, and praiseworthy? Or do they tempt us to comparison, insecurity, and shallowness of heart?

Smartphones and social media are incredibly addictive, but does that make them good? More and more people are becoming anxious when they leave their phones or are away from them for any amount of time. We allow them to interrupt thought, conversation, and solitude because they bring a kind of comfort.

According to the Anxiety and Depression Association of America, social media anxiety disorder is a real problem. They report nearly 20 percent of people with social media accounts cannot go more than three hours without checking them. With social media anxiety disorder, people who are away from their social media account for more than a few minutes begin to experience severe anxiety.

What does this, as a society, do to our ability to function as relational beings? Those without the disorder, who are just on their devices a lot—how does the distraction of a smartphone impair the ability to have conversation or to think deeply?

There is danger when social media sites start to become addictive, when they make us feel worse about ourselves or make us lonely. When we get anxious because we haven't checked our phones in minutes or hours is when we have to rethink how we are using them. When our Facebook usage increases our moral outrage but decreases our deep compassion for people as creations of God, we have to rethink how we are using it.

> When our Facebook usage increases our moral outrage but decreases our deep compassion for people as creations of God, we have to rethink how we are using it.

Stepping away from our phones, from artificial light, and spending time in real daylight can be a balm for our souls. Breathing deeply, away from our computers and accounts, can be refreshing and healing. Learning to have real conversation and real connection increases our empathy and our understanding of one another.

How does social media affect you? How do you feel when you are away from it? Is the way you use social media and think about yourself and others glorifying to God? I think using these questions to guide our usage is beneficial and powerful. The world needs people who are not afraid to turn off their screens.

CHAPTER 8

When I Need to Listen

John MacArthur defined peace as "the tranquility of the soul."

I find it interesting that the people in my life who live with this kind of tranquility are always good listeners. They seem to be able to live without trying to prove themselves, and because of that, they can give themselves fully over to others to listen.

And yet, listening is one of the most underappreciated attributes in our society. We live in a world of voices—so many voices that they threaten to overpower us, so we think the only way to combat them is to speak louder. Blogs, websites, and social media outlets are all platforms for us to speak and use our voice. This in and of itself is not a bad thing, but are we so focused on what we are saying that we forget to listen? And in what ways is this inability to listen affecting the peace in our souls?

When I was in graduate school, our professors mercifully made their classrooms technology-free zones. We wrote by hand and engaged in conversation. Phones were turned off or, better yet, left at home. And it freed us up to talk and to listen to each other in a way we wouldn't have otherwise because it gave us the space to *see* each other. This was invaluable for me as I worked on a master's degree in creative writing.

At the same time, I worked as a resident director in a college dorm. Many undergraduate students filled my apartment for meetings and events. Sometimes our meetings got to the point where I could not finish a sentence without several of them looking at their phones or being distracted and unable to continue a thought. I started asking them to leave their phones at the door, and this was met with tremendous anxiety and distraction. My students made it only a few minutes before looking at the buzzing basket, wondering which of them was getting a notification and what they were missing. It almost proved worse than allowing them to have their phones on hand.

With constant access to information, to the lives of other people, and to the digital platform of our own lives, anxiety in the United States has skyrocketed. Teenagers today are more connected and more anxious than ever before. And with this connectivity, with this ability to share only the parts of ourselves that seem worthwhile, it seems as though we've also lost the ability to really listen to one another. One might argue that now we are always listening—and that is true—but we are listening in pretty boxes; we are listening to compare; we are listening for our own gain.

> With this connectivity, with this ability to share only the parts of ourselves that seem worthwhile, it seems as though we've also lost the ability to really listen to one another.

On The Gospel Coalition's website, Dane Ortlund wrote an article, "Listen. It's a Ministry," about listening. In it, he said:

> To listen to someone, to really listen, is to break out of the prison of self-referentiality where we all tend to live. It's to get out of yourself—to leave Self behind. It's to hear

**what another says and resist the instinctive urge to map
it on to your own experiences and interpret accordingly.
It's far more than an auditory phenomenon; it's to shift
your focus from Self to another, to step into their reality,
to bear their life with them. It is, fundamentally, love.**

How often do we listen to really understand and not for our own
gain? How often do we find other people who will listen to us in this
way? How can we ever be vulnerable and real if we feel like we are
not listened to well? And if we don't have someone to listen to us,
how can we ever grow?

We all love to be around good listeners—I think because we
all love to share our stories. We want to be understood, and good
listeners offer that to us. I have learned a lot about friendship from
my once-a-month dinner club, but I have also learned about the art
of listening. Each one of those girls knows how to listen not just by
being silent but also by using their whole body. They lean in, they
make eye contact, and they ask follow-up questions. They make me
feel intensely *heard.*

There are other people I have felt this way with—my siblings,
my husband, my friends, and some of the women who mentor me.
Their ability to listen to me has profoundly shaped my life. Their
acts of compassion demonstrate to me that I am heard and what
I am saying is valuable. Those who have listened to me have made
me feel like my questions have value. They have encouraged me to
keep asking, to lean into my doubts and fears rather than away from
them.

Learning to listen seems to be something our world desperately
needs.

Listening to God

I wonder what it is about listening that we are afraid of. Is it the patience it requires? The quietness? Are we afraid about what we would learn about ourselves if we gave way to the silence?

Often, it is when I am anxious that I am most afraid of listening. I try to fill my mind and world with music, with blogs, with books, with movies—*anything* to keep my mind off the questions and the panic I'm feeling. I have wondered, in my calmer moments, what listening—inviting God into my fears and questions and then being willing to sit with it all—would do for my anxiety, my understanding, and my faith.

Galatians 5:22–23 addresses the fruit of the Spirit as love, joy, peace, patience, kindness, goodness, faithfulness, gentleness, and self-control. In church growing up, we seemed to treat these fruits as separate—asking what fruits we had been given and what fruits we needed to work on. But the Bible says the *fruit* of the Spirit. They all go together. When we have the Spirit in us, we don't have access to one fruit and not another. They aren't mutually exclusive of one another. The more we know and love God, the more He does His redeeming work in us, and the more we grow in the fruit of the Spirit.

> The more we know and love God, the more He does His redeeming work in us, and the more we grow in the fruit of the Spirit.

This was a huge realization for me. For years I thought love, joy, patience, and gentleness might be within my reach, but that peace, or the tranquility of the soul, was just not possible. I thought I would never be given peace and I would never be able to live without anxiety caused by my questions. I thought I would never be able to truly feel *safe*.

I realized I read the Bible the way I scroll social media. What could I cherry pick? What could I convert for my own personal gain? What would make me feel good? What were the quick fixes that would make me feel safe? I read verses out of context and without considering the big picture. I read verses to try to make sense of a specific situation in my life rather than understand it as a book about a God who stretches further across time and culture than we can fully comprehend.

There is such a danger in reading verses out of context, in inserting our own meaning onto them, and in only half listening to what the Bible says. As Jen Wilkin so beautifully puts it in her book *Women of the Word*, "The heart cannot love what the mind does not know." Until we understand the Bible, meditate on it, and truly yield to what it says, we cannot love its pages *or* be transformed by them.

All kinds of strategies and coping methods exist for dealing with anxiety. I cannot speak to the clinical methods, as I myself have not experienced clinical anxiety. My anxiety is a deep unsettling of the soul that comes from questions and experiences I cannot reconcile. So for me, the two most redemptive methods for speaking into my anxiety have been reading through the Bible comprehensively and *Lectio Divina*, which I will explain later. Both of these have involved learning to slow down and listen.

Reading through the Bible

When Andrew and I decided to start reading the Bible together, we began by looking for a reading plan. With our eggs and coffee each morning, we played the Bible on audio. That year quickly became one of the most transformative for us in so many ways.

We read it that first time solely for comprehension, to understand the big picture. We read through the Old and New Testament at the same time so that we were learning about creation as we read about Christ's birth and about Isaac on the altar as we read about Christ's death on the Cross. It was incredibly powerful to gain an understanding about what events took place when, about how each part of the Bible speaks to another. We witnessed God's heart for the hidden and the unseen and His compassion for His people. We learned about His justice, His mercy, and about how Christ truly is the fulfillment of the law.

Verses we had memorized as children and stories we heard in isolation suddenly took on new meaning as we understood them in light of the Bible as a whole. And there was plenty in there that still confused us, that I am sure we will return to again and again as we look for understanding, but the comprehension we've gained from reading everything for ourselves has been invaluable. This practice in listening—in coming to the Word without expectations, without trying to fit our theology into the passages, has given me a better understanding of the heart of God. That, in turn, has been incredibly helpful in inviting Him into my fears and anxieties.

First Peter 5:7 says, "Cast all your anxiety upon him because he cares for you." After reading through the Bible, I believe God truly does care for me, much more than I did before, because I read about the way God sees orphans and widows, the way He cares for the oppressed, the way He loves His people Israel through it *all.*

Andrew and I are about to head back into the Bible to read through it again. I know this act of imperfect listening will never be complete, but I also know each time I quiet my soul and open God's Word, He will meet me there.

> I also know each time I quiet my soul and open God's Word, He will meet me there.

Lectio Divina

Another listening method, which has been immensely helpful for me in coping with anxiety, is *Lectio Divina.* The Latin term for "divine reading," *Lectio Divina* is a repetitive, meditative way of reading Scripture. It is a way of quieting oneself enough to listen to Scripture and sit in the silence. This way of reading has challenged me to slow down, to read to understand rather then to check off a list. *Lectio Divina* has challenged me because of my natural inclination to run from silence, but I have learned through it that sitting in the silence is incredibly nourishing to my soul.

Andrew and I are in a discipleship group with about ten other men and women we have come to love deeply. We meet every other week, starting out with a delicious, home-cooked meal by our host, and then we move to the living room. We pull out our Bibles and begin by reading through a passage *Lectio Divina* style. This truly helps us to quiet our hearts and minds for the lesson ahead and helps us to read the Bible slowly and carefully.

There are several steps to *Lectio Divina*. It begins by slowly and reflectively reading a passage of Scripture. This first reading is done mainly for comprehension.

The passage is read a second time, more meditatively. What is the passage saying? What word or phrase in the passage jumps out to you?

The third time the passage is read, we think about the invitation to us in that passage. What are we being invited into? What is our response?

The fourth time through, we rest. We rest in the Word of God, put aside our words, and we make room for the silence. This silence, I think, is the most transformative part: allowing ourselves the time and space to *listen* to everything we just read.

The thing about the Word of God is that it is living and active, sharper than any double-edged sword. So the Word, when we take the time to listen to it, *will* change us. The change may be slower than we hoped, less visible than we hoped, and different from what we hoped, but the change *is happening* because Jesus has promised to not give up working in us. We can trust that as we read and as we listen.

> The Word, when we take the time to listen to it, *will* change us.

If you've never done *Lectio Divina* before, here are some great passages to get started with, especially as you work through and understand your own anxiety and where it comes from.

Psalm 1	Matthew 8:23–27
Psalm 3	Ephesians 3:14–21
Psalm 46	Philippians 4

Many of these verses are ones I have committed to memory. I find them incredibly useful when I find myself in panic-filled situations. When I feel anxiety creeping over me, and along with it the inability to listen, I recite these verses. Our bodies and minds need to hear truths, over and over again, about who God is and how He loves us.

Listening to Nature

Almost every summer growing up, my family took a trip to Algonquin Provincial Park in Ontario, Canada.

The night before we would leave, we always slept restlessly, counting the hours, trying to cool ourselves down with the fan, the car all packed, and canoes strapped to the top. Freeze dried food had been lined up in white garbage bags marked as breakfast, lunch, or dinner, squeezed and rolled up into packs alongside sleeping bags, quick dry towels, and one outfit change.

We went out to find quiet, or maybe to quiet ourselves enough to listen. We loaded up our belongings on our backs and carried canoes through the woods, put in on lakes, paddled through lilies, through grassy swamps, through deep waters. At night we put up our tents and boiled water for hot chocolate and beef stroganoff, eaten straight out of the package with a fork rinsed off in the lake. Then we sat around the fire and listened to the rhythmic splashing of the lake onto the shore of our campsite, to the haunting echo of the loon's cry across the water, to the crackle of the fire, the scurry of the chipmunks and squirrels across the pine needle floor around us. We listened to the murmur of one another's voices as we lay back and looked at the stars, brighter there than anywhere on earth. It was on these trips we learned about how my parents fell in love. We talked about what it means to be human, and we laughed and found new things to love about each other because we removed the distractions.

During the days we paddled and hiked, miles and miles, and it was in the silence of the paddling that we heard how much there was to listen to. We listened through touch of the water as we dipped our paddles in. We listened to the birds, to the shape of the clouds, to the soft munching of the moose hidden deep in the swamp. Listening in Algonquin takes me out of myself completely, even as I experience so richly the wonder of the world around me. Listening makes me expand, in a way. It is a perspective shift. It is the realization that the Lord made them all too.

One year in particular, I remember being afraid to go to Algonquin. I was afraid of being in the wilderness, which is rational—there had been a nasty bear attack earlier that year that had killed a family. I was more afraid, though, of the silence. You can't bring phones or computers into the wilderness, and that year, because of my anxiety, because of questions I didn't want to face, I had spent a lot of time numbing my mind with technology and distraction. When I had a hard time falling asleep at night, I watched movies, read magazines, or slept with my phone next to me just so I would have some form of light to reach for.

I was afraid to come into the silence (Or was it the loudness?) of nature, to be confronted with my own thoughts without escape. Wendell Berry talks about the peace of the wild things, but I was so afraid of the wild things. I was afraid to be alone.

What I discovered that trip was how *good* it was to be in the silence, as hard as it was to adjust to it. It was good for me to have a hard time falling asleep, to lay there until the frantic cycle of my thoughts finally slowed enough for sleep to come. It was good in the days following to be so exhausted from hard work that I was asleep minutes after hitting the forest floor of roots padded with pine needles, my sweatshirt as a pillow. It was good to listen to the loon and hear the cycles of nature from dawn to dusk, and then through the night, to be reminded that all of this exists without my thought or will. What did it teach me about God, at this time when I was too afraid even to come to Him with my questions? That the world is far bigger than my understanding, that God holds every one of those stars I see, and He also knew to give me the sisters and brother that lay next to me. That God provides for the squirrel and the bird and the fox and the moose, and He has always provided for me. That this earth is bursting full of gifts: gifts of smell, touch, taste, sight, if I will listen for them. The complex mind that created this wilderness I walk through is understanding enough to develop an entire universe, and I am created alongside the rest of it. So that is something to hold to.

When I get anxious, sometimes a walk is the best thing for me because it pushes me to listen again. It reminds me that I am small but significant, that the whole world is currently being tended to, and my heart will be tended to as well.

> I am small but significant. The whole world is currently being tended to, and my heart will be tended to as well.

Listening to One Another

One of the most influential books I read this year was *The Gospel Comes with a House Key* by Rosaria Butterfield. She talks about the importance of practicing hospitality in a way that shares the gospel with our neighbors. "Our post-Christian neighbors need to hear and see and taste and feel authentic Christianity, hospitality spreading from every Christian home that includes neighbors in prayer, food, friendship, childcare, dog walking, and all the daily matters upon which friendships are built."

I love this quote because I feel it embodies the way it looks when we choose to listen to our neighbors rather than try to be heard. Bake a cake, mow someone's lawn, or drop by with flowers. Isn't this a form of listening as well—showing others we hear and see them?

I read *The Gospel Comes with a House Key* as a new mom, at the same time that I was studying the Book of James with a group of women from church. James talks about loving the orphan and the widow out of love for Jesus and His love for us. I wanted to do that, but my life seemed so restrictive with a baby. In the past, I had volunteered quite a bit. Before June was born, I taught ESL classes to immigrant moms and creative writing classes at nursing homes. When I had my daughter, I hoped to continue doing these things, but all my free time seemed to be hidden behind a pile of laundry and a million dirty diapers. We tried to volunteer at a nursing home until flu season got so bad we were turned away each week.

I felt anxious about my lack of service, like I wasn't a good Christian or I was doing something wrong. I began to think subconsciously that God was looking down on me because I was not doing enough to serve him. I began to think that I would be *useful*— to God and to the world around me—after my children grew up and moved away.

I think during this time, I forgot a crucial part of the Christian life. Romans 8:15 says, "The Spirit you received does not make you slaves, so that you live in fear again; rather, the Spirit you received brought about your adoption to *sonship*. And by him we cry, 'Abba, Father.' The Spirit himself testifies with our spirit that we are God's children" (emphasis added).

I don't think I am the only one in the church who tends to view myself more as a servant than a child. And as a servant, I think I must *do*. I must be in Bible study. I must volunteer. I must make meals and give money. When I think in this mindset, I think that I must *do* listening as well, that hospitality to my neighbors is something I can check off a box.

But before we are called to serve, God calls us *children of God— heirs*. We are coheirs with Christ to His eternal riches. We have been loved with an everlasting love. We are called, first and foremost, to love God and to enjoy Him. We are called to invite Him into our lives and to *rest* in the work He has done on our behalf. We have been *heard* in the most intimate and complete way possible. He is the God who hears, and His ears are turned toward *us*.

Listening to those around us—extending a welcoming spirit of hospitality—is far more about who we are and who we become when we view ourselves as sons rather than servants. We can listen without expecting anything, without trying to prove anything, and without needing to justify anything. We see

> We can listen without expecting anything, without trying to prove anything, and without needing to justify anything.

ourselves as people who have been loved fully—so we can listen fully to others. We don't listen to check off a box. We do it because we are *children of God.* Knowing this, for me, takes away so much of the anxiety that comes with doing.

Rosaria Butterfield's book challenged me to understand that God never gets the address wrong. He placed my growing family and me in a specific neighborhood and community. He gave me specific gifts and talents that play out in this community just by living my life. Loving our neighbors isn't something we do—it is weaved into the way we live our life, *because we are children of God.*

You may read in Scripture, or hear people refer to, God calling His children *sons.* But note, the use of the word *son* does not leave out the word *daughter.* Galatians 3:28 says, "There is neither Jew nor Gentile, neither slave nor free, nor is there male and female, for you are all one in Christ Jesus." God gives us the same rights the firstborn son held in Hebrew tradition. Because of what Jesus did for us, we are all granted the status of firstborn sons, coheirs with His inheritance.

Because I am an heir and child of God, because I have been forgiven a great debt, because I have been *heard,* I am able to listen to others. I am free to stop thinking about how I can be effective *outside of* my role as a wife and mother and instead consider how I am effective *through* it. As my status as *child of God* has allowed me to relax enough to listen rather than need to be heard, to extend a hospitable spirit toward others, I realize I extend the gift of listening because I have been listened to—and also that extending the gift of listening is a gift to me.

> I extend the gift of listening because I have been listened to.

When we listen to another person, we are let in a little bit to their souls, their inner rooms. We are able to put together a more complete picture of who they are. Many times, for me, this is a worshipful experience, as I start to understand how complex and layered God made each person. It also provides us an opportunity to show the other person they are heard and they are valuable, the way we have been shown that. Sometimes we are also given information that we can take to our heavenly Father in prayer. Sometimes people speak into the work being done in my own life, and it is an encouragement to listen to that. We are called to carry each other.

When I became I mom, I thought my listening days were over. Would I ever have an undistracted conversation again? But God has used my daughter to open up countless doors for conversation with new people. Conversations are distracted and disjointed, but I think there is something about a baby that gives people room. And so in that way, my daughter, who doesn't yet feel any tension between servanthood and sonship, is a lovely gift.

It is in this time, when I find myself both busier and more still than I have ever been, that God is showing me the gift I give others by listening. He is filling my home and my messy kitchen with a beautiful stream of visitors, prompting me to make some coffee, sit down for a minute at a time, and offer myself to others—not as a form of duty but because I am a son.

He is also showing me the gift he gives *me* as he teaches me to listen. How does listening help my anxiety? It forces me to slow down, to see outside myself, to try to understand the life of another. It reminds me that none of us has all the answers but that there are treasures to be found in every person. He's allowed me to see the work He is doing in the lives of others. As I stumble through learning this art, I see the work being done on my soul. The *doing* of listening does not make me more complete. I listen because I trust the work God is doing in me. I trust that He hears.

CHAPTER 9

When I Need Communion

I let the ball of dough drop so that it landed with a satisfying smack on the wooden table, sending flour-like puffs of smoke into the air and onto my clothes. I pushed and kneaded the soft ball, realizing how nice it is to sink my hands into something real. I looked out the open window above my sink inside the servants' quarters of this old mansion where I live and wondered how many people kneaded bread on this old counter before me, wondered what kind of lineage I entered into by the act of rolling and pulling, of creating nourishment for someone else.

Jesus referred to Himself as many things, but as I read through the Book of John, the reference to Jesus as bread is what stands out. I tend to read John a lot. When I begin to feel too anxious or like I am starting to drown in theology, when I begin to get muddled by my questions and start waking again in the night, I turn to John. I love the way the book is written, and it is good for my soul to start again with the actual words Jesus said. When I read John, I feel, in a strange way, *held*. It may not answer all my questions, but it teaches me about the one who *can* and maybe one day *will* answer them, and I think that does me a great deal more good than having everything handed to me.

My feet pressed gratefully against the cold tile of the floor as I kneaded on that hot June day. It was ten in the morning, and the air was already thick with humidity that swam around the old apartment so that the wood expanded and dampened to catch it. I kneaded and pulled the bread across the table, thinking about the preparation, the meditation, the forethought that goes into fresh bread, into consuming it at a meal. Good bread is a food that cannot be rushed, and I have a feeling Jesus is the very best kind.

Why did Jesus choose bread? He hints at it, throughout the Book of John. He told His disciples, when they urged Him to eat something, "I have food to eat that you know nothing about. . . . My food . . . is to do the will of him who sent me and to finish his work" (John 4:32–34). When He had a crowd of five thousand listeners who needed something to eat, Jesus asked Philip, "Where shall we buy bread for these people to eat?" (John 6:5). And then He provided it from so little—from within Himself. He called Himself the bread that comes down from heaven—the *living bread*. If anyone eats of this bread, he will live forever. Jesus said, "This bread is my flesh, which I will give for the life of the world (v. 51).

I set my bread in my tin bowl and put it on the windowsill to rise, to allow the yeast and the warm air to do their work until it is finally ready to bake in the oven.

Bread and wine. This is the way Jesus talked about Himself. Life-giving, rich, tasteful nourishment: a feast. In John 2, Jesus' very first miracle, He provided a large amount of the very best wine at a party, and there was enough to go around. As one of His last acts on earth, Jesus fed His disciples with bread and wine. "This is my body given for you; do this in remembrance of me. . . . This cup is the new covenant in my blood, which is poured out for you" (Luke 22:19–20). Jesus nourished His disciples. He said, I am your feast. I am life.

This is our communion: practicing resurrection.

The Living Water

The final drops of the sweet hymn echoed across the sanctuary, wringing out their words and notes like rain on a thirsty people. The bread broken, the wine poured out, everyone went to the table.

Oh, for a thousand tongues to sing, my great Redeemer's praise.

Jesus said to the woman at the well that He had water, and if she drank from it she would never thirst again. Has anyone never thirsted again? I drink and the next day I am thirsty. I am so thirsty. Where is this water He's talking about?

If I had a thousand tongues, sometimes I wonder if I would use them for praise. I have one tongue now, and I seem to use it for quite a few other things. My tongue is my most constant reminder that I am broken, and the way I use it becomes a shackle more often than not. If I had a thousand tongues, I don't think I could bear the weight of what I would do with them.

But then again, if I could find this living water, maybe I would want a thousand tongues. Maybe it would take me that many tongues to even begin to express the praise inside me.

The words of this hymn fall all across this sanctuary, on all the thirsty people. Some people put up umbrellas to shield the words, to keep them from soaking skin and soul. Others tilt their heads back and lap that water up. I remember a season when I watched this happening and felt like the rain wouldn't touch me. I was lost in scorching sun, in anxiety and frustration, and while it rained all around me, I was all dried up. I wondered then if I would use a thousand tongues to praise a God whose whisper I could not feel.

If only I were certain. If only I were sure I could be forgiven, that hope would not disappoint me. I looked down at my hands that could not have been made by accident, and I doubted.

Where was God, in that season for me, when I was so thirsty and could not find water? When my questions piled up around me, kept me up at night, and I could not answer them? Was He still there, just as close? Was it still raining, and I could not feel it? How did I miss the flood?

Here is what I love about communion: there is always space at the table. The table encompasses not only us but all the sin and brokenness, the unfulfilled longing, and the unmet expectation that come with us. None of it, and none of us, are turned away. We walk forward, to the table, carrying our own weight, our shame, our hurt, our doubt, and what does God do? He says take and eat. We are weary travelers, and He does not admonish us for being so tired. He nourishes us. He says, My body was broken for you and for this so that you have the promise of becoming whole.

> There is always space at the table.

That is the mercy of God, that when we feel far from him, He never turns away. When we question and doubt, when we are anxious because we cannot feel his presence, He is not offended, and He doesn't give up on us. He doesn't say, *enough already*, and throw up his hands. One of the characteristics of God is that He is faithful. He cannot go against himself. He cannot be unfaithful.

All that time I questioned, I wondered what was wrong with me that my faith was so weak. I wondered, if God was real, what would He think about me questioning like that? Now I know that not only did God not look down on me, He *used* those questions purposefully, skillfully, to teach me. I look back on those questions now and I realize they were not an inconvenience, or a test, or wrong, or an annoyance, or any of the things I thought they were at the time. The questions made me think about my faith in a way I might never have otherwise. They pushed me to look for answers, to read my Bible, to memorize Scripture, to start discussions, to sit in the *not knowing*. Why couldn't I *feel* God's presence? Why couldn't I understand things like suffering or hell or sin or love? Probably because if I could, or if I thought I could, I would have been content with a half-thought-out faith and a half-lived life. The questions were the avenue by which my faith finally grew.

> After the Lord Jesus had spoken to them, he was taken
> up into heaven and he *sat* at the right hand of God.
>
> —Mark 16:19 (emphasis added)

I thought a lot during this time about Jesus sitting. Jesus *sat* at the right hand of God not because he was lazy or tired, but He sat with an air of completion. He *sat* because His work was finally done. It was complete. I thought about Jesus sitting and was reminded again about the God who is not linear.

When I was born, Jesus didn't stand up and scurry around to get to work again on my heart. He didn't clasp His hands together and say, "Oh, I've got my work cut out for me with this one!" And when I began asking questions, when I began to wonder if this faith was true enough to stake my life and eternity on, Jesus didn't start to scurry around and say, "One more job to do, I better sort her out," or worry about when I was finally going to get my act together. He wasn't pacing the floor thinking, "*When* is Rachael going to *finally* understand this?"

What Jesus accomplished and completed is *completely done.* Philippians 1:6 says we can be *confident* that "he who began a good work in you will carry it on to completion until the day of Christ Jesus." So this work is being completed and is *already* complete, somewhere in eternity, because Jesus *sits.* Jesus is outside of time— He is and has already completed the work necessary for both my salvation and my sanctification. I can be confident that one day I *will* know hope complete and full because Jesus is not trying to get His act together. He *sits.*

All that time that I doubted, that I wondered, that the questions kept me up and I felt shaky talking to anyone else about them because they patched me up with not-quite-theologically-correct answers, I kept taking Communion. I kept lining up with the thirsty people, and I kept asking for rain for my soul. I said, "Jesus, I cannot *feel* You, but I am trusting that somehow, someway, you are near, and these questions are for my good." And what did Jesus give me?

> I kept lining up with the thirsty people, and I kept asking for rain for my soul.

I realize now that He gave me so much.

He gave me bread and wine, a church with good teaching, a community of believers to work out my faith and questions with, and his unfailing Word. What He gave me all that time was *food* and *drink,* the promise of living water, until I could finally start to untangle and make sense of a few of my thoughts.

Every week, I stood in that line as words and rain fell around me, and I wondered if God could really forgive a heart as obtuse as mine, if there really was a place for me at the table. But there is nothing anyone can say or do that would exclude them from this table. I can't come to Jesus with my knowledge because my knowledge isn't good enough. We come to Jesus empty-handed, with only outstretched arms to offer, and He fills them with Himself. He says, "Eat of this hope; drink of this promise. I have food to eat you know nothing about."

And I began, over time, to think that even I could be forgiven.

The rain didn't fall on me all at once. There has been no flood of water, no surge, no riptide of certainty that has erased all my doubt. But I have noticed things, a little at a time, in myriad tiny specks splattered onto dry soil that taste like hope. I noticed Andrew, rocking on the porch, as we stared into the parking lot of the university where we lived, at the streetlights you can imagine are fireflies if you squint and tilt your head a little. I noticed myself, sitting next to him with a book, both of us silently listening to the crickets fiddle and sing somewhere among the trees. I noticed the last golden light of the sun and how it made the trees grow shadows across the pavement. I noticed the smell of barbecue chicken and smoke from the grill and wondered how many days, in the history of the world, had ended like this one? *Day after day they pour forth speech; night after night they display knowledge.* G. K. Chesterton wrote about the repetitive nature of God in his book *Orthodoxy*:

> Because children have abounding vitality, because
> they are in spirit fierce and free, therefore they want
> things repeated and unchanged. They always say, "Do it

again"; and the grown-up person does it again until he is nearly dead. For grown-up people are not strong enough to exult in monotony. But perhaps God is strong enough to exult in monotony. It is possible that God says every morning, "Do it again" to the sun; and every evening, "Do it again" to the moon. It may not be automatic necessity that makes all daisies alike; it may be that God makes every daisy separately, but has never got tired of making them. It may be that He has the eternal appetite of infancy; for we have sinned and grown old, and our Father is younger than we.

The idea that God might not get bored with making daisies or with waking up the sun every morning, in ushering in seasons or directing the birds as they sing, made me think that maybe God does not get bored with people who ask questions. Maybe He delights in them, maybe he even created me *to* ask questions, so that He could answer them again and again with joy. Maybe with every day, He says, "Look at that! Look at the sun, up in the sky, again! Listen to the song of the birds, specific to every kind!"

For me these moments—of living water hitting parched soil—look like when our feet developed blisters and our legs grew tired from walking fourteen miles, but Andrew and I dragged our legs and our sunburnt skin just a mile farther to the St. Mary's pub. We celebrated this island, the shifting landscape, our family, my nephew born the day before on the other side of the world, my sister who birthed him, and my mom and grandmother whose stories about this place made us want to come back and explore it. We ate full plates of sausage and fries and it felt like our lives were full of beauty and blessing, of varied scenery like what we had seen that day, of meadows and cliffsides and sheep grazing in utter peace. We reminisced about the day and enjoyed the gift of sitting, of feeling full, of being like cozy door mice tucked away in an old stone wall. We talked of old life, of new life, of the God who is constantly making all things new.

They also look like when we moved to a new place and city, away from our friends and the lives we had built to start a new one, and we braced ourselves for another visit to a new church. We prepared for awkward conversation, or worse, no conversation, but it didn't happen like that at all. At the door of the church we were welcomed like old friends, talked to for a long time, invited for lunch. We were brought in, folded in, to what would become some of the richest community we have known. The people who have enveloped us at the church Andrew and I attend have truly loved us well. They brought us meals, rocked our baby, invited us into their homes and became a part of our lives.

Mostly, though, I think these drops hit the parched soil of my soul every time I take communion. Maybe the drops bounced off the soil a little, but they hit the same spot, for years, until one day I woke up and realized I had been watered. One night, when I was eight or nine, I became so afraid of the future, the unknown, about sickness and what happens after death. My dad came in and took me over to my second story bedroom window. He said, "Pretend I'm holding you outside this window in a fireman's grip, and

> Maybe the drops bounced off the soil a little, but they hit the same spot, for years, until one day I woke up and realized I had been watered.

you're dangling by just one arm. What if you got tired and let go? What would happen?"

I looked at him and at the window. "Nothing," I answered. "Because you would still be holding me."

"And as your dad," he said, "would I look at your hand, see that you got tired, let go, and just walk away?"

"No," I said. I knew he loved me too much to drop me.

Communion has been a tangible reminder of this fireman's grip God has on me. In all this time, He has never let me go. Instead, every week, He leads me to the table where I am fed. I line up with other believers on Sunday mornings at church and am reminded, *the body of Christ for your brokenness. The Blood of Christ to fill in all your gaps. The hope of the Resurrection and rich inheritance.*

This act of communion is the living water and eternal bread.

After rising for most of the day, the bread is finally ready to bake. I set our oven to four hundred degrees and have to leave the kitchen because of the heat. I set the table with my flowery china and pick some fresh hydrangeas from the garden. Andrew comes home from work and turns on the grill for the marinated pork and summer vegetables. Our friends arrive, and we make our way into the old dining room—these are friends with whom the conversation is always full and rich, equal parts listening and sharing. We pass the piping hot bread around the table, break it, allow the butter to melt into it, and we feast on it. Slowly, I am starting to grasp what it means, as I feast in my heart on the Bread of Life, as I learn to come forward every Sunday to be nourished, to be reminded that Jesus paid it all. There's a joy baked into that bread and into these friends and into my faith that rings true in all my questions.

CHAPTER 10

When I Need to Find My Place

I had a dream about the gift of place, and when I woke up, laying in the silence and comfort of the blankets, of the fan blowing overhead and the birds all chattering in the early morning light, my first thought was that He knows where I am.

I pulled my pregnant body out of bed and shuffled to the living room where I sat with my Bible and my pen for a while to think about this idea. While my husband and baby slept and the day came to life around me, I read about how God gives His people a city where they can settle. He lifts the needy from the ash heap. In Psalm 116 He fulfills promises and delivers His children. In Psalm 139, He has searched us and knows us—when we sit and when we rise, when we go out and lie down. Where can we go from His spirit?

Jesus saw Nathanael under the fig tree, and He saw all the Samaritan woman had done. Four days dead, he was able to see Lazarus and call Him back. Acts 17 says He determines the exact times set for every person and the exact place where He will live (v. 26).

Right before Jesus died, He gave Mary and John to each other as mother and son. One of His last acts was to make sure the people He loved were accounted for, to give them the gift of place.

When my anxiety comes, it is usually triggered by the idea that the world is too big and I am too small, and I feel insignificant and out of control. I feel unknown and unaccounted for, like I could slip away from my body and into nothingness, like maybe my soul and my body are not quite tethered.

In a lot of ways, the anxiety I feel in general is the fear that I do not belong. Don't we scroll social media for affirmation? Don't we retreat in our friendships when we feel left out? Don't we subconsciously use food, marriage, technology, and religion as a method of belonging?

On that morning though, it felt as though God took that fear, allowed me to sit in it, and then woke me up out of the blue to show me that He gives His people the mercy of place. I am accounted for, and I am held, wherever I am. If I go into the depths, He is there. If I rise up onto the wings of the eagles, He is there. He saw Nathanael under the fig tree, and He sees me this morning. He is a God who promises so many times in Scripture that He will hold and bind His people together.

We've worked so hard, especially in America, to make life about the individual—about being the smartest, the fastest, the best—and I wonder if we have missed somewhere the value of just *belonging*— to the earth, to God, to one another. That is, after all, the hope of the gospel—we who were once outsiders now *belong*, are now heirs of a great inheritance. We who were once far off have now been made near. We are now called *a child of God*—the ultimate way of belonging and being known.

> That is, after all, the hope of the gospel—we who were once outsiders now belong, are now heirs of a great inheritance.

As eternal souls sewn up into individual bodies, it makes sense that place would be so important to us. Our feet are tied to gravity, and our bodies are tied to this space and time. We nourish them with food we grow from the ground, and the people we love and know best are the ones we grow up with. We use place as a means of marking identity, value, and heritage.

Because we are so bound to place, it makes sense that a God who is not at all bound by it would use place as the center of so many Bible stories. God creates the heavens and the earth, plants for land, and plants for water. He gave Adam and Eve the garden to cultivate and nurture. When they were banished from the garden, they were banished from a place. When God called Abraham He called him out of a place he knew and into a new place, but He was with him. While Abraham left the place he knew, he never left the place where he was *known*—because *God accounts for our places.*

The redemptive story of Israel is God restoring them to the Promised Land and then opening up a way for Jews and Gentiles alike to enter God's ultimate promised land. Jesus told His disciples there are many rooms in His house. He knows our need for a physical, tangible place, and He provides it for us.

We cannot escape the God who sees. God saw Hagar and her son. God saw Tamar, abused by two husbands. God saw Rahab, and Mary, and Paul. And *God sees us.* God sees our current place—He sees us in our homes and jobs, our friendships, our disappointments, our hopes, our dreams. God sees our current place, and He also sees our future place—and every time we take communion, He reminds us of that place we have at the table with Jesus, wholly forgiven, wholly accounted for. One of the greatest gifts we have been given is that of place.

May this mercy of place wash over us all.

Benediction

I'm sitting in the cozy corner of a bakery in the snowy state of New York eating a lemon-blueberry scone and watching locals pile in and out in groups, alone, for here, to go. There is a lipstick stain on my white coffee cup—one of those stains that goes through an industrial dishwasher and becomes an indelible mark, a permanent stain. I wonder who drank from this elixir of the gods before me, how she took it: with milk, cream, sugar, or straight, bitter black. The shade of the lipstick is a deep enough pink to make me think she is in her late forties, early fifties, and I wonder if she was meeting a friend, or a sister, or if she came in by herself to escape for a few hours in a good book. It is the same shade of lipstick my mother wears, and I wonder if maybe this was her cup, if she came to meet with a friend and talk about her children, and now I am drinking from the same one.

I watch these little pieces of community file in and file out and all I can think is, so what? So what if we can recite words of Scripture, if we can ask questions—if our anxiety is here to stay, through all of that?

What difference does it make, if it does not rid us of the thing we most want to be rid of?

When the Jacob of Genesis prepared to meet his twin brother after years apart—the twin whose birthright and blessing Jacob stole, the twin Jacob fled from after being threatened with his life—he prayed to God for deliverance. Genesis 32 tells the story about how Jacob finally acknowledged that deliverance, this time, would be in

God's hands and not his own. After years of trying to control his own fate—his livelihood, his blessing, his wives—Jacob realized his redemption was out of his reach.

That night, Jacob wrestled with God, and God gave Jacob a limp. He touched his hip socket and dislocated it. Jacob asked for deliverance and in return, he got a disability.

Why did God do that? Jacob was asking for help. Why would God *wrestle* with him and then put his hip out of joint?

As my view of God gets bigger, why do my questions grow as well? Why aren't they pushed away?

Why do I also have a limp?

It would be easy for us to look at the promises of Scripture as a cure-all. *This will fix all my problems if I can apply it to my life.* We forget David was hunted by Saul, that Paul was put in prison, and that Jesus was put to death on a Cross.

What I am saying is I believe Scripture to be true. And I believe God works *everything* for the good of those who love Him.

I also believe He may never take away my questions.

It is this *un*knowing that keeps me asking questions. It is the awareness of how much I don't know, and how much I know there is to be afraid of, that keeps me looking for answers. And it is through my anxiety that I am beginning to grasp a fraction of the way God loves me.

Maybe the limp showed Jacob what *could* have happened. Maybe it was a sign God would be always with him.

I will take this limp of anxiety if it will teach me the way I am loved.

John 11 tells the story of Lazarus's death. When Lazarus's sisters, Mary and Martha, sent Jesus word—"Lord, the one you love is sick"—Jesus heard the news and said Lazarus wouldn't die (vv. 3–4). He heard Lazarus was sick, and He didn't come running. Jesus stayed right where He was.

Doesn't that seem as though He doesn't really care? What person hears about an illness of someone they love and does nothing? But when Jesus does go to see Lazarus, He tells His disciples that Lazarus has already died. He knows what has happened.

I love reading about Martha's relationship with Jesus, about her response. She says to Jesus, "If you had been here, my brother would not have died. But I know that even now God will give you whatever you ask" (vv. 21–22).

Martha, in her time of crisis, had unwavering faith in Jesus. She didn't understand why Jesus didn't come earlier. She didn't understand why her brother had to die. But she knew that even after death, Jesus still had ultimate power over the body and soul of her brother.

Jesus had great compassion on Martha. He knew she didn't understand. He told her, "I am the resurrection of the life. The one who believes in me will live, even though they die; and whoever lives by believing in me will never die. Do you believe this?" (vv. 25–26).

And Martha said *yes*.

Martha probably still had questions. She was at the beginning of her grief. And yet she answered, "Yes, Lord; I believe that you are the Christ, the Son of God, who is coming into the world" (John 11:27 ESV).

Then Jesus called her brother from the tomb, and Lazarus walked out alive.

It is amazing to me that Jesus didn't ask Martha to sort out her questions before she came to him. And Martha didn't say—I believe, *but* there is so much to figure out. Martha just said yes, Lord, I believe. In the midst of my grief, my suffering, my questions, I will say I believe.

Jesus knows my questions, but He does not shoulder me with the burden of answering them. He just asks, *do you believe?*

Here are my questions, Lord.

Here are my doubts.

Here are my fears.

And yet—*yes,* I believe.

Here is the place of grace unmeasured.

> **My people will live in peaceful dwelling places, in secure homes, in undisturbed places of rest.**
>
> **—Isaiah 32:18**

All of us love to feel safe. We love life's comforts because they are pleasant and because they make us feel in control. I love to fill my home and days with friends, clothes, hobbies, and food that make me feel safe and in control. We mistake these comforts for peace.

Haven't we all felt like Henny Penny at some point in our lives? Haven't we all watched the sky fall? We've lost things, people, comfort, security, and suddenly, our lives don't feel like they've got a shred of peace in them. How is it possible to have peace when the sky has fallen—when *the worst thing* has happened and our lives don't look at all the way they were supposed to?

Isaiah 32:18 strikes a deep chord with me. This promise is the essence of my heart's desire: a peaceful, secure home, an undisturbed place of rest, a place where the sky could never fall. The Lord makes this promise to Israel in a time of suffering and turbulence, amid the foretelling of what would be *the worst thing*—exile and oppression—right before the *best thing*—the coming of Christ and His new kingdom.

Through Christ's birth, life, death, and Resurrection, He gave us *the best thing*—salvation, hope, and reconciliation. He conquered every worst thing, meaning there is no scenario, no circumstance, over which He is not Lord. Because of the Cross, we bear only a shadow of death, sickness, and pain because Christ bore the brunt and conquered it all, and all suffering can do to us in this life is draw us closer to Him. He is our secure dwelling place, our undisturbed place of rest, our promise that because He lives, the sky will never truly fall.

Maybe this verse can change our perception of *the worst thing*. Maybe the worst thing isn't to suffer, to experience loss, to be uncomfortable, to be afraid. Maybe the worst thing is to live a life in which we are never made aware of the depth of our fall, the extent to which we are loved, and the hope strong enough to look at the sky falling before us and feel only peace within us.

> Maybe the worst thing is to live a life in which we are never made aware of the depth of our fall, the extent to which we are loved, and the hope strong enough to look at the sky falling before us and feel only peace within us.

God is our refuge and strength, an ever-present help in trouble. Therefore we will not fear, though the earth give way and the mountains fall into the heart of the sea, though its waters roar and foam and the mountains quake with their surging.

—Psalm 46:1–3

When anxiety rises up inside me—when I realize I do not have answers to questions or control over the safety of my life or the lives of those dearest to me—that is when I turn to the psalms. It is there I repeat, rhythmically, to the breaths in my chest that defy all pattern, that I trust in the Lord, who turned my wailing to dancing, whose love reaches to the heavens, who will fulfill His purpose for me, who will redeem my life and take me to Himself.

Maybe we are anxious because we ask too much of ourselves. God does not ask me to conquer my anxiety. When the earth of Psalm 46 gives way, when the mountains fall into the sea, He does not ask me to stop them quaking. He only asks that I be still, and know He is God. He only asks that I seek refuge in Him, for He is a mighty fortress.

I know no greater love than this.

Conclusion

Last spring Andrew and I flew to Charleston, South Carolina, with our four-month old baby. One morning we decided to pack lunches, get in our rental car, and drive along the beach until we could find a place to park and walk. It was a gray day, with just enough cloud coverage, and we walked for miles, hand in hand, following the line of the ocean.

What have I learned about the ocean, in the past few years? It is unknowable, to some degree. It is vast, untamable, full of wonder, mystery, chaos, and terror. But the ocean is not uncontrolled.

There are many more questions to answer; many more fears for me to work out, but I know that I am not walking through them alone. I am held in the fireman's grip; I am lifted up by my community; I am slowly starting to see myself as I actually am.

Maybe I wasn't made to understand the ocean. Maybe, as the ocean steadily erodes the sand, its Maker is refining me. I cannot conquer the ocean—it is far too big and too powerful. But the ocean and I were stitched and sewn together, made by the God who hovers.

Darkness thrives on making you feel alone. This journey of my life, though it has felt dark at times, has become a slow, step-by-step pattern of walking into the light: of finally starting to see myself for who I am. I am not unredeemable. My anxieties are not too big for God. His disposition toward me is one of a Father to a child, and this whole walk I'm on is grounded in love.

My whole life, I pray, will become a repetitive step into the light, a shutting out of the dark. I pray this for my family, for my community, for the church, and the world. When we live in light, we make the darkness shrink back.

We must keep doing this, until it crumbles.

Study Guide/Discussion Questions

Chapter 1: The Questions, the Gift, and the Promise

The author talks about receiving anxiety as an unexpected gift. What are some unexpected gifts you have received in your life? How have you come to view them as gifts?

How has anxiety shaped your ability to ask questions? What kind of questions have you asked as a result of your anxiety?

Chapter 2: When I'm Anxious about God

Have you struggled to believe God is good? How have you worked through that?

How have you seen God's faithfulness as you ask questions about his character?

Name a time in your life when you have seen or come to understand more about God's goodness.

What role has the church played in your walk with anxiety and doubt? How can you encourage the church to become more supportive of those walking through anxiety?

Chapter 3: When I'm Anxious about My Marriage

Are you married? If so, how has the reality of marriage proved different from what you expected? If not, what expectations do you hold for your marriage?

How has your spouse helped you through hard times in your life?

What ways can you practically love your spouse for who they are today? How can you encourage them in who they will become?

Chapter 4: When I'm Anxious about Motherhood

What are some of the ways you worry about your children?

How can you hold and claim God's promises for your children?

What ways can motherhood teach you about God's character?

Chapter 5: When I'm Anxious about My Calling

Have you worried about your vocation? How did you choose the vocation you are in?

How does the way the Bible addresses calling shape your own view of it?

How can you move forward confidently in your career choice?

Chapter 6: When I'm Anxious about My Friendships

What ways do you combat or invite loneliness in your life?

In your friendships, do you act like a person worthy of time and love?

How can you remind yourself and encourage others that in Christ we are all enough?

How can you be a good friend to those in your life prone to anxiety and worry?

Chapter 7: When Social Media Makes Me Anxious

Are you on social media? How often?

What is your relationship like with social media? How does it impact your mood, friendships, and lifestyle?

Chapter 8: When I Need to Listen

What makes a good listener?

Who are the people in your lives who are good listeners? How has their ability to listen been a gift to you?

How can we become better listeners?

Do you tend to "cherry pick" the Bible? How do you think that affects your ability to listen to it as a whole book?

Practice Lectio Divina. How was the experience for you? What did you learn or observe?

Chapter 9: When I Need Communion

The author talks about experiencing communion as a place where we are all invited in. How have you experienced communion?

What has been an anchor in your life during times of doubt or wondering?

What is the significance of communion?

Chapter 10: When I Need to Find My Place

How does place shape who we are and who we become?

Why does it matter that God knows our places?

If you enjoyed this book, will you consider sharing the message with others?

Let us know your thoughts at info@newhopepublishers.com. You can also let the author know by visiting or sharing a photo of the cover on our social media pages or leaving a review at a retailer's site. All of it helps us get the message out!

Twitter.com/NewHopeBooks

Facebook.com/NewHopePublishers

Instagram.com/NewHopePublishers

New Hope® Publishers is an imprint of Iron Stream Media, which derives its name from Proverbs 27:17,
"As iron sharpens iron, so one person sharpens another."

This sharpening describes the process of discipleship, one to another. With this in mind, Iron Stream Media provides a variety of solutions for churches, missionaries, and nonprofits ranging from in-depth Bible study curriculum and Christian book publishing to custom publishing and consultative services. Through the popular Life Bible Study and Student Life Bible Study brands, ISM provides web-based full-year and short-term Bible study teaching plans as well as printed devotionals, Bibles, and discipleship curriculum.

For more information on ISM and New Hope Publishers, please visit

IronStreamMedia.com

NewHopePublishers.com

OTHER NEW HOPE
BOOKS YOU MAY ENJOY

**UNSHAKABLE
PURSUIT**
ISBN: 978-1-62591-545-0

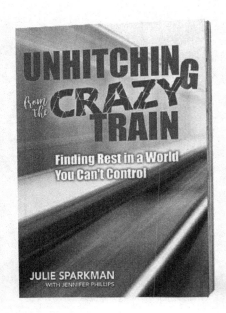

**UNHITCHING
FROM THE
CRAZY TRAIN**
ISBN: 978-1-62591-536-8

VISIT NEWHOPEPUBLISHERS.COM FOR MORE DETAILS